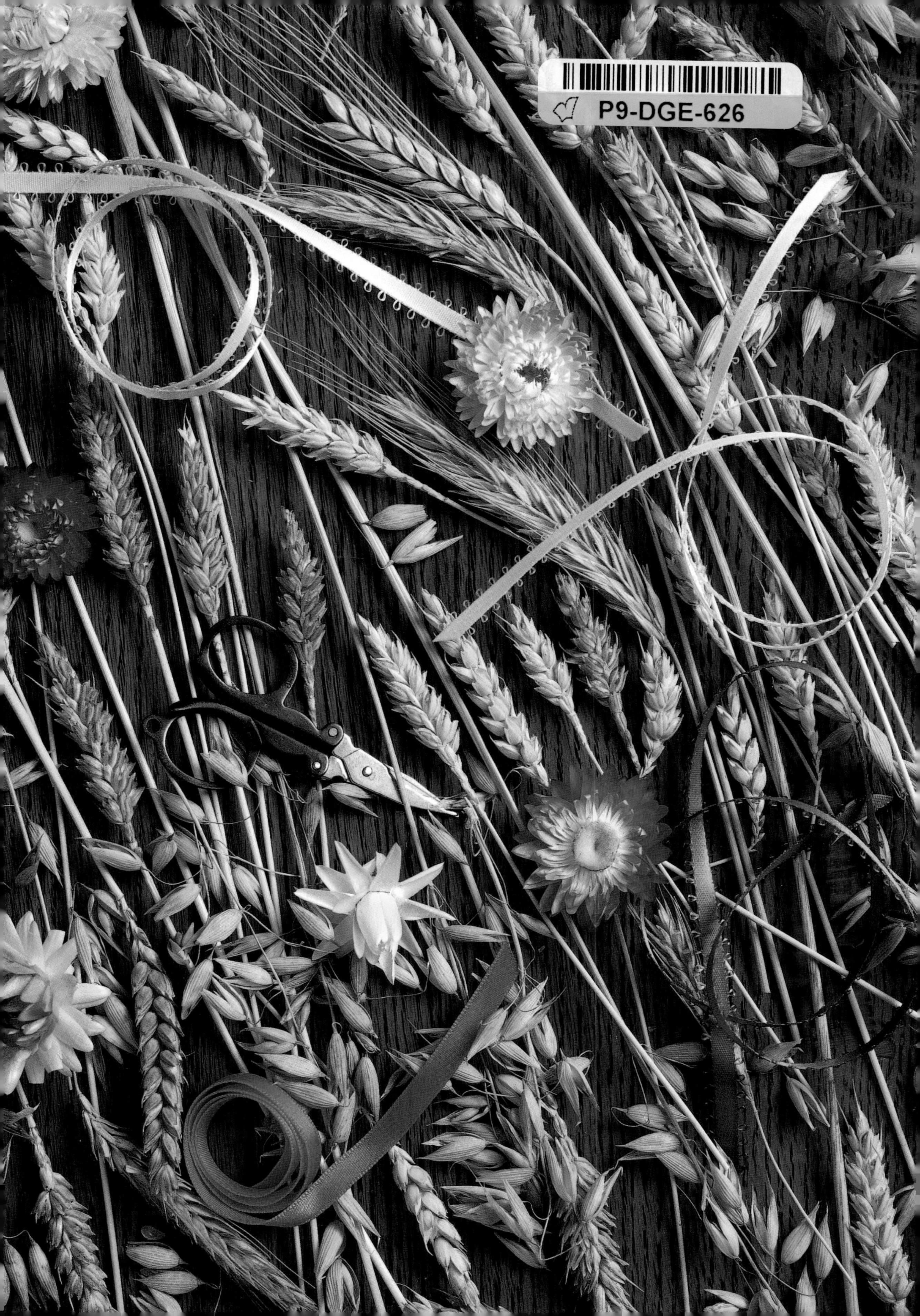

IV

THOUSAND YEARS OF WOMEN'S POETRY

The voices that would not be stilled

— *Edited by Fiona Pagett* —

CHAUCER PRESS
LONDON

Published by Chaucer Press
an imprint of the Caxton Publishing Group
20 Bloomsbury Street
London WC1B 3JH

ISBN 1 904449 07 7

Designed and produced for Chaucer Press
by Savitri Books Ltd

MAISONS A L'ENTRÉE DU VILLAGE BY JEAN CHARLES CAZIN, 1841-1901.

CONTENTS

WOMEN'S POETRY

PICKING CABBAGES, ANTON MAUVE 1838-1888.

INTRODUCTION

Why, you might ask as you pick up this book, an anthology of women's poetry? In these days when equality is the watchword in almost every walk of life, is this not sexist, divisive and reinforcing stereotypes that we should have left behind us long ago?

Perhaps. But perhaps also the interest in this collection lies in the fact that most of the poems included here were written long before the days of equal opportunity, some of them by women who were forbidden formal education not just by the unwritten rules of the society in which they lived, but by law. Some were written by women who had no opportunity to travel outside the town where they were born; still others by women of aristocratic birth who nevertheless had to conform to the restricted role that society allowed them. A number of the medieval poems are the work of nuns – women who were denied (or who voluntarily denied themselves) even the normal social intercourse of their secular sisters.

But all the poets in this collection show an intelligence, a willingness to think and to challenge, a concern for the human condition and for personal happiness, and often a sense of humour, that ranks with anything produced by the less hamstrung male poets.

It is largely but by no means entirely true that throughout the centuries female poets have tended to write about 'feminine' subjects. Love, family, nature, religion, life and death, and life after death have been their predominant themes. When they have taken up social issues, at least until the twentieth century, they have been concerned more with the suffering of the poor on the streets – the personal, human element – than with broader causes.

Interestingly, the main exceptions to this somewhat sweeping rule are to be found in Ireland, where women's pens have long been as powerful, as political and as vitriolic as men's. By the nineteenth century, black women in America were also taking up a cudgel carried into our own times most notably by Maya Angelou; and Emma Lazarus was an early fighter for Jewish causes.

Interestingly, too, women have always had a subversive streak. Constrained before marriage to wait passively for male advances and after marriage to endure male imperfections uncomplainingly, they seem to have been painting a jaundiced picture of love and the unreliability of men almost since poetry began. The medieval folk songs from India included here are humorous, even bawdy – a tradition that has survived to this day. In *In His Books* E. Nesbit – brought up in inhibited Victorian times, although her own private life was admittedly unconventional – goes one step further, referring daringly to a wife's infidelity.

This is not to say that women's poetry lacks deep feeling. Indeed, women – perhaps because so many of them were constrained to spend much of their time sitting at home without much to do – have often written movingly, even inspiringly, on the subject of death and the hereafter. Emily Brontë facing her own death and Charlotte Brontë mourning the death of both her younger sisters are just two examples of great courage in the face of tragedy. Emily Dickinson and, more recently, Marianne Moore, led noticeably quiet lives which in no way diminished their creativity or their poetic genius.

In short, women have written in all sorts of ways on all sorts of subjects. There is something in this collection to make every reader laugh, cry or merely have pause for thought.

❧❧

WOMEN'S POETRY

SAPPHO (7th century BC)

One of the earliest known female poets, Sappho was born on the Greek island of Lesbos, whose women were reputed to be the most beautiful of the ancient world. Her poetry, though it survives only in fragments, is famous for its passion – an inseparable mixture of adoration from afar and intimate sexual yearning. However, as these extracts show, her emotions did not always get the better of a certain dry wit and wisdom.

He is like a god, that man
Facing you, leaning over to be close,
He smiles, and, alert and glad, listens
To your mellow voice

And quickens in love when you laugh.
That pierces my breasts, jolts my heart
If I dare the shock of a glance.
I cannot speak,

My tongue sticks to my dry mouth,
Thin fire spreads beneath my skin,
My eyes cannot see and my aching ears
Roar in their labyrinths.

Chill sweat slides down my body,
I tremble, I turn greener than grass.
Not living nor yet dead, I cry
From my tormented limbo.

❧❦❧

But I endure, even this painful love.

∂▲∂

Someone, I'm bold enough to say,
Will remember us
In times to come.

∂▲∂

Wealth without moral splendour
Is a dangerous neighbour;
But join the two together:
There is no greater fortune.

∂▲∂

When fury rages in the breast,
Watch that reiterating tongue.

Hildegard of Bingen (1098-1179)

Born into a noble family, Hildegard became a religious recluse at the age of eight and a
nun at about fifteen. She lived most of her long life at the convent of Disibodenberg, in
the Rhineland of what is now Germany, where she became abbess in 1136. Most
unusually for a woman of her time, she travelled throughout Germany
to preach and became known as a mystic and prophet.
As with Teresa of Avila (see page 26), her early writing was inspired by visions
and she later produced a collection of religious songs which are still widely sung and
recorded today. The second piece quoted here is an extract from The Play of the Virtues,
the earliest medieval morality play, in which the 'characters' are the embodiment
of various qualities that make up a human being.
All in all, Hildegard's achievements mark her as one of the most
remarkable women of the Middle Ages.

Songs for Saint Disibod (extract)

O green strength of the hand of God,
where He has planted a vineyard,
it shines in the heights
like a stately column,
You are glorious as you prepare for God.

And O mountain on high
you will never weaken in God's testing
but you stand apart like an exile.
No man in armour has the power to seize you.
You are glorious as you prepare for God.

Opposite: The Annunciation. Miniature from the *Hours* of Anne de Bretagne.

Glory be to the Father and to the Son and to the Holy Spirit
You are glorious as you prepare for God.

Ɂ❧Ɂ❧

THE PLAY OF THE VIRTUES (extract)

The Virtues
We virtues are in God

and remain in God.

We fight for the King of kings

dividing good from evil.

We appeared at the first battle

and won the victory,

while he who wished to soar too high fell to the ground.

And so we fight now

and come to the aid of all who call on us:

we trample on the wiles of the devil

and we lead those who wish to follow us

to the blessed mansions.

The complaint of the souls, trapped within the flesh
We wanderers!

What have we done, straying into sins?

We should have been the daughters of the King

but fell into the shadow of sin!

O living Sun,

bear us on your shoulders

into that most just inheritance

which we lost in Adam!

O King of kings,

we fight in your battle.

Prayer of the faithful soul

Sweet divinity,

delightful Life

in which I will wear a bright garment,

accepting what I lost at my first appearance,

I sigh for you, and I invoke all the virtues.

The virtues

Happy soul,

beautiful creature of God,

you are formed in the most profound wisdom of God,

you express love in great measure.

The faithful soul

Oh let me come to you with joy,

that you may grant me the kiss of your heart.

Virtues

Daughter of the King,

we must join you in the fight.

The Soul, dejected, laments

What sore distress, what a heavy weight

I bear in the garment of this life,

since it is too hard for me to fight against the flesh.

᠔♠᠔

The easy juxtaposition of the sacred and the profane, the passionate love for God or that of a human lover is a recurrent theme in Indian poetry of that period. Many poets of that era were simple people who plied small trades. Sule Sankavva stands out, however, as she was a prostitute. This apparent conversation with a client becomes fascinating when it is realised that the woman is addressing her plea to God/Shiva – the libertine.

SULE SANKAVVA (12th century)

IN MY HARLOT'S TRADE

In my harlot's trade
having taken money from one man
I daren't take it from a second, sir.
If I do,
they'll stand me naked and
kill me, sir.

And if I cohabit
with the polluted,
they'll cut off
my hands and nose and ears
with a red-hot knife, sir.

Ah, never, no,
Knowing you I will not.
I vow it,
promiscuous Shiva.

৯৶৯

18

JANABAI (c. 1298-1350)

CAST OFF ALL SHAME

Cast off all shame,
and sell yourself
in the marketplace;
then alone
can you hope
to reach the Lord.

Cymbals in my hand,
a veena on my shoulder,
I wander about;
who dares to stop me?

The pallav of my sari
falls away (A scandal!);
yet will I enter
the crowded marketplace
without a thought.

Jani says, My Lord,
I have become a slut
That I may reach Your home.

ঌঌ

WOMEN'S POETRY

Women's poetry from medieval India is often robust and earthy, the defiant cry of the oppressed who yet manages to find enjoyment from life and has the strength to mock her 'betters'. This folk song containing advice on how to survive as a daughter-in-law – the traditional family drudge – is typical of this oral poetry .

ANONYMOUS FOLK SONGS

IF YOU KEEP AWAY FROM YOUR HUSBAND'S ELDER BROTHER

If you keep away from your husband's elder brother
and are pleasant to your father-in-law
we will be able to say you are the worthy daughter
of a noble landowner.

A stranger takes the young daughter from her mother.

If you are the first to take your bath, the last
to eat, we shall be able to say you are
truly the daughter of a deserving father.

A stranger takes the young daughter from her mother.

If you serve everyone with milk and rice
and content yourself with rice alone
we shall be able to say you are the proper
daughter of a wise father.

A stranger takes the young daughter from her mother.

OPPOSITE. FRESCO OF A LADY, BUNDY PALACE, RAJASTHAN.

YOU REARED ME TO BE A CAREFREE BIRD, O MOTHER

You reared me to be a carefree bird, O Mother
You counted the days till I could fly, O Mother
Now the cage is bare without a bird, O Mother
Without me your home is empty, O Mother
Who shall urge me to eat, O Mother
Who shall wake me from sleep, O Mother
Who will feel the longing of my heart, O Mother
For they shall only exaggerate my words, O Mother
And they shall make fun of them, O Mother
Oh their harsh words I cannot bear, O Mother
They shall flay my skin to the bone, O Mother
Oh how I was afraid of the dark, O Mother
But now I have freed you from my care, O Mother
And when the first hibiscus blooms, O Mother
Darkness shall reign on your hearth, O Mother
The camel drinks with its long neck, O Mother
But you have none to caress, O Mother.

THE *TULSI* PLANT (HOLY BASIL) IS TENDED
BY HINDU WOMEN AS A SYMBOL OF THE
GODDESS LAKSHMI.

The courts of medieval Japan produced a number of women poets who occupied prominent positions in society and were influential in both the political and the literary fields. The woman now known as Nun Abutsu became a Buddhist nun on the death of her husband. She was one of the first Japanese writers to depict nature in a realistic fashion, a legacy which would influence Japanese literature through the ages.

Nun Abutsu (c. 1240-1283)

On my way home
in the dark hours before dawn,
the gathering clouds
began to drop their showers –
on my sleeves, first of all.

As you went away
in the dark hours before dawn,
leaving me behind,
the tears I sent after you
could well have caused that shower.

Kyogoku Tameko (died c. 1316)

To the sound of the wind
it adds the refreshing notes
of its own cool voice:
a stream down in the valley
in the shade of the dusky hills.

A WINTER POEM

Following the wind,
hail falls in a sudden burst –
passing quickly by;
then again, from between the clouds,
light spills from the moon.

JUSAMMI CHIKAKO (flourished c. 1290-1310)

A SPRING POEM

In the first light of dawn,
the wind from my window
strikes with a chill;
but wait, it must be spring –
for I catch the scent of plum.

EMPRESS EIFUKU (1271-1342)

It is the breezes
and time marching ever onward
that we should resent –
the blossoms themselves
feel no desire to fall.

I hear it in the wind
and see it among the clouds
gathering at dusk –
the relentless advance
of autumn's melancholy.

WOODBLOCK PRINT BY SUZUKI HARUNOBU, SHOWING THE SEMI-LEGENDARY
NINTH-CENTURY POET, ONO NO KOMACHI.

St Teresa of Avila (1515-1582)

Teresa of Avila, who was canonised in 1622, spent most of her life in a Carmelite convent and is remarkable for the writing inspired by her mystical visions. Her prose works described both her physical journey to found new convents and reform the Carmelite Order, and the spiritual journey towards mystical ecstasy as the bride of Christ. The language she uses in her verse bears a remarkable resemblance to the conventions of conventional love poems, though in this case the object of her passion is divine rather than human.

Prayer

The arrow with which He wounded me
Was barbed around with love,
And so my spirit came to be
One with its Maker, the Lord above.
No love but this I need to prove:
My life to God surrender'd is
And my Beloved One is mine
And I at last am surely His.

I Am Thine, and Born for Thee

I am Thine, and born for Thee:
What wilt Thou have done with me?
Sov'reign Lord upon Thy throne,
Endless Wisdom, One and Whole,

Goodness that dost feed my soul,
Good and great, One God alone:
Vile Thou seest me, yet Thine own,
As I sing my love for Thee.
What wilt Thou have done with me?
Thine I am, for Thou didst make me;
Thine, for Thou alone didst save me;
Thine – Thou couldst endure to have me;
For Thine own didst deign to take me.

ANNE BRADSTREET (1612-1672)

Considered to be the first English poet – of either sex – in America, English-born Anne
Bradstreet emigrated at the age of eighteen with her husband, a non-conformist minister
who became Governor of Massachusetts. Her religious poetry reflects the Puritan tradition
in which she was reared, sacrificing the pleasures of this life in readiness for the next.

THE FLESH AND THE SPIRIT

In secret place where once I stood,
Close by the Banks of Lacrim flood,
I heard two sisters reason on
Things that are past, and things to come;
One Flesh was call'd, who had her eye
On Worldly wealth and vanity;
The other Spirit, who did rear
Her thoughts unto a higher sphere:

Sister, quoth Flesh, what livest thou on
Nothing but Meditation?
Doth Contemplation feed thee so
Regardlessly to let earth go?
Can Speculation satisfy
Notion without Reality?
Dost dream of things beyond the Moon
And dost thou hope to dwell there soon?
Hast treasures there laid up in store
That all in th' world thou count'st but poor?
Art fancy sick, or turn'd a Sot
To catch at shadowes which are not?
Come, come, I'll shew unto thy sense,
Industry hath its recompense.
What canst desire, but thou maist see
True substance in variety?
Dost honour like? Acquire the same,
As some to their immortal fame:
And trophyes to thy name erect
Which wearing time shall ne'er deject.
For riches dost thou long full sore?
Behold enough of precious store.
Earth hath more silver, pearls and gold,
Than eyes can see, or hands can hold.
Affect's thou pleasure? take thy fill,
Earth hath enough of what you will.
Then let not goe, what thou maist find,
For things unknown, only in mind.

SPIRIT: Be still, thou unregenerate part,

Disturb no more my settled heart,

For I have vow'd (and so will doe)

Thee as a foe, still to pursue.

And combate with thee will and must,

Untill I see thee laid in th' dust.

Sisters we are, yea twins we be,

Yet deadly feud 'twixt thee and me;

For from one father are we not,

Thou by old Adam wast begot,

But my arise is from above,

Whence my dear Father I do love.

Thou speakst me fair, but hatst me sore,

Thy flatt'ring shews I'll trust no more.

How oft thy slave, hast thou me made

When I believ'd, what thou hast said,

And never had more cause of woe

Then when I did what thou bad'st doe.

I'll stop mine ears at these thy charms,

And count them for my deadly harms.

Thy sinfull pleasures I doe hate,

Thy riches are to me no bait,

Thine honours doe, nor will I love;

For my ambition lyes above.

My greatest honour it shall be

When I am victor over thee,

And triumph shall, with laurel head,

When thou my Captive shalt be led,

How I do live, thou need'st not scoff,

For I have meat thou know'st not off;

The hidden Manna I doe eat,

The word of life it is my meat.

My thoughts do yield me more content

Then can thy hours in pleasure spent.

Nor are they shadows which I catch,

Nor fancies vain at which I snatch,

But reach at things that are so high,

Beyond thy dull Capacity;

Eternal substance I do see,

With which inriched I would be:

Mine Eye doth pierce the heavens, and see

What is Invisible to thee.

My garments are not silk nor gold,

Nor such like trash which Earth doth hold,

But Royal Robes I shall have on,

More glorious then the glistring Sun;

My Crown not Diamonds, Pearls, and gold,

But such as Angels heads infold.

The City where I hope to dwell,

There's none on Earth can parallel;

The stately Walls both high and strong,

Are made of pretious Jasper stone,

The Gates of Pearl, both rich and clear,

And Angels are for Porters there;

The Streets thereof transparent gold,

Such as no Eye did e're behold,

A Chrystal River there doth run,

Which doth proceed from the Lamb's Throne.

Of Life, there are the waters sure,

Which shall remain for ever pure,

Nor Sun, nor Moon, they have no need,

For glory doth from God proceed:
No Candle there, nor yet torch light,
For there shall be no darksome night.
From sickness and infirmity,
For evermore they shall be free,
Nor withering age shall e'er come there,
But beauty shall be bright and clear;
This City pure is not for thee,
For things unclean there shall not be:
If I of Heaven may have my fill,
Take thou the world, and all that will.

Sor Juana Inés de la Cruz (1651-c1691)

In an age when women were not admitted to universities, Sor Juana Inés de la Cruz was a remarkable scholar, scientist and musician. Despite being reprimanded for her scholarship, she amassed Mexico's finest library. She was also the most admired Spanish American poet of her day, sometimes described as Mexico's tenth Muse.

Stop, Shadow of My Elusive Beloved

Stop, shadow of my elusive beloved,
image of enchantment that I most desire,
beautiful illusion for whom I happily die,
sweet fiction for whom I painfully live.

If to the magnet of your graces, attractive,
my breast serves as obedient steel,

why do you capture my love in such pleasure
if you are to leave me later, fugitive?

But you cannot boast, satisfied,
that your tyranny triumphs over me:
for though you have eluded the tight noose

that encircled your fantastic form,
it matters little to deceive arms and breast
if I fashion a prison for you in my fantasy.

VERSES
*against the inconsequence of men 's taste and strictures, when they
attack those qualities in women of which they are themselves
the cause*

Stupid men, who unreasonably attack women,
without seeing that you are the cause of the very thing you blame;

if with unparalleled ardour you make love to their disdain,
why do you expect them to act virtuously when you incite them to sin?

OPPOSITE. THE GENEAOLOGICAL TREE OF THE GUZMAN FAMILY IN THE CONVENT
CHURCH OF ST DOMINGO IN OAXACA, MEXICO. THIS MAGNIFICENT COLONIAL
BUILDING WAS ERECTED BETWEEN 1551 AND 1666.

SANCIYA HONNAMMA (LATE 17TH CENTURY)

The most remarkable thing about this Indian poet is that she should have written poetry at all: she was a servant in a royal palace at a time when only the most privileged of either sex had leisure to write. Her thinking was traditional and her most famous work is called Duties of a Devoted Wife, *but as this extract shows she was not unaware of the plight of some women.*

SONG OF A MARRIED WOMAN (extract)

Wasn't it woman who bore them?
Wasn't it woman who raised them?
Then why do they always blame woman,
These boors, these blind ones?

In the womb, they're the same.
When they're growing they're the same.
Later the girl will take, with love, what's given.
The boy will take his share by force.

For money's sake, for trust
And friendship's sake
Don't give a girl to a walking corpse
Bereft of virtue, youth and looks.

Don't say, 'We're poor people, where
Can we get jewels from?'
Instead of spending on yourself
Provide your daughters with clothes and ornaments.

A LADY OF THE MUGHAL COURT PLAYING THE VEENA, LATE SEVENTEENTH CENTURY.

ESTHER JOHNSON (1681-1728)

The details of the connection between Esther Johnson (nicknamed 'Stella') and the eighteenth-century literary and intellectual giant Jonathan Swift remain obscure, but it was certainly an close one and they may even have been married. They met in about 1696, when he would have been twenty-nine and she sixteen, and they remained close until her death. His Journal to Stella *(1701-13) is a fascinating record of his life in London, but also a clear indication of the intimacy that existed between them. This affectionate poem shows that, whatever else had happened between them, Stella regarded Swift as a mentor – and that she had a ready wit and strong intelligence of her own.*

STELLA TO DR SWIFT
on his birth-day, November 30, 1721

St Patrick's Dean, your country's pride,
My early and my only Guide,
Let me among the rest attend,
Your pupil and your humble friend,
To celebrate in female strains
The day that paid your mother's pains;
Descend to take that tribute due
In gratitude alone to you.

When men began to call me fair,
You interposed your timely care:
You early taught me to despise
The ogling of a coxcomb's eyes;
Showed where my judgment was misplaced;
Refined my fancy and my taste.

Behold that beauty just decayed,

Invoking Art to Nature's aid:

Forsook by her admiring train,

She spreads her tattered nets in vain;

Short was her part upon the stage;

Went smoothly on for half a page;

Her bloom was gone, she wanted Art

As the scene changed, to change her part;

She, whom no lover could resist

Before the second Act was hissed.

Such is the fate of female race

With no endowments but a face;

Before the thirtieth year of life,

A maid forlorn or hated wife.

Stella to you, her tutor, owes

That she has ne'er resembled those;

Nor was a burthen to mankind

With half her course of years behind.

You taught how I might youth prolong

By knowing what was right and wrong;

How from my heart to bring supplies

Of lustre to my fading eyes;

How soon a beauteous mind repairs

The loss of changed or falling hairs;

How wit and virtue from within

Send out a smoothness o'er the skin;

Your lectures could my fancy fix,

And I can please at thirty-six.

The sight of Chloe at fifteen
Coquetting, gives me not the spleen;
The idol now of every fool
Till Time shall make their passions cool;
Then tumbling down Time's steepy hill,
While Stella holds her station still.

O! turn your precepts into laws,
Redeem the women's ruined cause,
Retrieve lost empire to our sex,
That men may bow their rebel necks.
Long be the day that gave you birth
Sacred to friendship, wit and mirth;
Late dying may you cast a shred
Of your rich mantle o'er my head;
To bear with dignity my sorrow,
One day alone, then die tomorrow.

੪੬੪

OPPOSITE. THE BAY OF DUBLIN. JONATHAN SWIFT, STELLA'S 'MENTOR', WAS BORN AND
EDUCATED IN DUBLIN.

LADY DOROTHEA DUBOIS (1728-1774)

The eighteenth century in England was a time of gaiety and wit – among the aristocracy, at least. This cheerful poem by a largely forgotten poet satirises the social strictures under which young ladies of the time were placed.

SONG

A scholar first my love implor'd,
And then an empty titled Lord,
The Pedant talked in lofty strains,
Alas! his Lordship wanted brains:
I listen'd not, to one or t'other,
But strait referr'd them to my Mother.

A Poet next my love assailed,
A Lawyer hop'd to have prevailed;
The Bard too much approv'd himself,
The Lawyer thirsted after pelf:
I listen'd not, to one or t'other,
But still referr'd them to my Mother.

An Officer my heart would storm,
A Miser sought me too, in Form;
But Mars was overfree and bold,
The Miser's heart was wed to gold:
I listen'd not to one or t'other,
Referring still unto my Mother.

And after them some twenty more,

Successless were, as those before;

When Damon, lovely Damon, came,

Our hearts straight felt a mutual flame:

I vow'd I'd have him and no other,

Without referring to my Mother.

FANNY GREVILLE (18th century)

Another poet who is rarely read today, Fanny Greville's experience of love was apparently less happy than that of Dorothea Dubois.

PRAYER FOR INDIFFERENCE

Ask no kind return of love,

No tempting charm to please;

Far from the heart those gifts remove,

That sighs for peace and ease.

Nor peace nor ease the heart can know,

That, like the needle true,

Turns at the touch of joy or woe,

But, turning, trembles too.

Far as distress the soul can wound,

'Tis pain in each degree:

'Tis bliss but to a certain bound,

Beyond is agony.

CAROLINE SOUTHEY (1786-1854)

The second wife of the poet Robert Southey, also known by her maiden name of Bowles, Caroline spent much of her life in the New Forest in a constant struggle against poverty. She married Southey, a lifelong friend, only four years before his death, to the enormous resentment of his children. She was never a very successful writer, but this verse has a appealing gentle poignancy.

I NEVER CAST A FLOWER AWAY

I never cast a flower away,
The gift of one who cared for me
A little flower – a faded flower –
But it was done reluctantly.

I never looked a last adieu
To things familiar, but my heart
Shrank with a feeling almost pain,
Even from their lifelessness to part.

I never spoke the word 'Farewell,'
But with an utterance faint and broken;
An earth-sick longing for the time
When it shall never more be spoken.

FELICIA HEMANS (1795-1835)

Felicia Hemans was the most commercially successful poet of her day, though her work is perhaps a bit sentimental for some modern tastes. She was also extraordinarily prolific. 'Casabianca', more usually known by its first line, 'The boy stood on the burning deck', commemorates the thirteen-year-old son of an admiral at the Battle of the Nile in 1798, who remained at his post and died when his ship finally exploded.

CASABIANCA

The boy stood on the burning deck
Whence all but he had fled;
The flame that lit the battle's wreck
Shone round him o'er the dead.

Yet beautiful and bright he stood,
As born to rule the storm –
A creature of heroic blood,
A proud, though child-like form.

The flames rolled on – he would not go
Without his father's word;
That father, faint in death below,
His voice no longer heard.

He called aloud: – 'Say, father, say
If yet my task is done!'
He knew not that the chieftain lay
Unconscious of his son.

'Speak, father!' once again he cried,

If I may yet be gone!

And but the booming shots replied,

And fast the flames rolled on.

Upon his brow he felt their breath,

And in his waving hair,

And looked from that lone post of death

In still yet brave despair;

And shouted but once more aloud,

'My father! must I stay?'

While o'er him fast, through sail and shroud,

The wreathing fires made way.

OLD SAILING SHIPS IN THE PORT OF DUBLIN.

They wrapt the ship in splendour wild,
They caught the flag on high,
And streamed above the gallant child
Like banners in the sky.

There came a burst of thunder-sound –
The boy – oh! where was he?
Ask of the winds that far around
With fragments strewed the sea! –

With mast, and helm, and pennon fair,
That well had borne their part;
But the noblest thing which perished there
Was that young faithful heart!

ELIZABETH BARRETT BROWNING (1806-1861)

Elizabeth Barrett is best known for the romance surrounding her love affair with and eventual marriage to the poet Robert Browning, who was six years her junior and whom she met when she was nearly forty. Elizabeth's domineering father deeply disapproved of the relationship and the couple eventually eloped to Italy, where they spent most of the rest of her life. In her lifetime she was considered a greater poet than her husband – her name was even put forward as a possible Poet Laureate when William Wordsworth died in 1850 (it is interesting to note that there has never yet been a female Poet Laureate). She was a passionate supporter of such issues as Italian unity and the abolition of slavery, though her political works were less popular than her lyrical and spiritual poems.

SONNETS FROM THE PORTUGUESE (two extracts)

Unlike are we, unlike, O princely Heart!
Unlike our uses and our destinies.
Our ministering two angels look surprise
On one another, as they strike athwart
Their wings in passing. Thou, bethink thee art
A guest for queens for social pageantries,
With gages from a hundred brighter eyes
Than tears even can make mine, to play thy part
Of chief musician. What hast thou to do
With looking from the lattice-lights at me –
A poor, tired, wandering singer, singing through
The dark, and leaning up a cypress tree?
The chrism is on thine head – on mine the dew
And Death must dig the level where these agree.

Go from me. Yet I feel that I shall stand
Henceforward in thy shadow. Nevermore
Alone upon the threshold of my door
Of individual life I shall command
The uses of my soul, nor lift my hand
Serenely in the sunshine as before,
Without the sense of that which I forbore –
Thy touch upon the palm. The widest land
Doom takes to part us, leaves thy heart in mine
With pulses that beat double. What I do
And what I dream include thee, as the wine

Must taste of its own grapes. And when I sue
God for myself, He hears that name of thine,
And sees with my eyes the tears of two.

TO GEORGE SAND: A DESIRE

Thou large-brained woman and large-hearted man,
Self-called George Sand! whose soul, amid the lions
Of thy tumultuous senses, moans defiance,
And answers roar for roar, as spirits can:
I would some mild miraculous thunder ran
Above the applauded circus, in appliance
Of thine own nobler nature's strength and science –
Drawing two pinions, white as wings of swan,
From thy strong shoulders, to amaze the place
With holier light! that thou to woman's claim,
And man's, mightst join beside the angel's grace
Of a pure genius sanctified from blame, –
Till child and maiden pressed to thine embrace,
To kiss upon thy lips a stainless fame.

TO GEORGE SAND: A RECOGNITION

True genius, but true woman! dost deny
Thy woman's nature with a manly scorn,
And break away the gauds and armlets worn
By weaker women in captivity?
Ah, vain denial! that revolted cry

Is sobbed in by a woman's voice forlorn: –
Thy woman's hair, my sister, all unshorn,
Floats back dishevelled strength in agony,
Disproving thy man's name! and while before
The world thou burnest in a poet-fire,
Through the large flame. Beat purer, heart, and higher,
Till God unsex thee on the heavenly shore,
To which alone unsexing, purely aspire.

BHABANI (early 19th century)

Bhabani was perhaps the most famous exponent of two important forms of folk entertainment in India, the tarja *(repartee) and the* jhumur *(song and dance). Their subjects were frequently subversive, and they came under fire with the rise of a prosperous middle class, who disapproved both of the songs and of the women who performed them.*

KNOCK KNOCK KNOCK

Knock knock knock
What a shock!
There's someone at the door.
In the middle of the night,
What a fright!

Listen!
Desire is calling me

SEVENTEENTH-CENTURY MINIATURE SHOWING MOGHUL LADIES ON A TERRACE.

Out into the dark.
I shan't look around,
Nor care if there's a sound,
To call me a sinner would be trite.

There's someone at the door
In the middle of the night,
What a fright!
Ram's really sweet,
Shyam's the same;
It's only my husband who's sour,
Too boring to suffer for an hour
Except when we're having a fight.
There's someone at the door
In the middle of the night,
What a fright!

Shyam's uncle's father-in-law
Is one hell of a man.
Jadu's cousin's brother-in-law
Now he's my latest fan.
Ma Mitter's got hysterical
Oh what an awful sight!
There's someone at the door
In the middle of the night,
What a fright!

કહ

CHARLOTTE BRONTË (1816-1855)

Charlotte Brontë, the eldest of the three famous literary sisters, best known for her novel Jane Eyre, *was the only one of the sisters to marry and the only one to live beyond the age of thirty. All three had unhappy experiences as governesses or teachers which coloured their writing. Their lack of commercial success as poets – only two copies of their collected poems were sold on publication in 1846 – turned all three sisters to novel writing, but their poetry is now widely read and highly regarded. Their passionate devotion to their home on the Yorkshire moors, most obvious in Emily's* Wuthering Heights, *recurs in the poems of all three sisters.*

SPEAK OF THE NORTH

Speak of the North! A lonely moor
Silent and dark and trackless swells,
The waves of some wild streamlet pour
Hurriedly through its ferny dells.

Profoundly still the twilight air,
Lifeless the landscape; so we deem,
Till like a phantom gliding near
A stag bends down to drink the stream.

And far away a mountain zone,
A cold, white waste of snow-drifts lies,
And one star, large and soft and lone,
Silently lights the unclouded skies.

❧❧❧

On the Death of Anne Brontë

There's little joy in life for me,
And little terror in the grave;
I've lived the parting hour to see
Of one I would have died to save.

Calmly to watch the failing breath,
Wishing each sigh might be the last;
Longing to see the shade of death
O'er those beloved features cast.

The cloud, the stillness that must part
The darling of my life from me;
And then to thank God from my heart
To thank Him well and fervently;

Although I knew that we had lost
The hope and glory of our life;
And now, benighted, tempest-tossed,
Must bear alone the weary strife.

On the Death of Emily Jane Brontë

My darling, thou wilt never know
The grinding agony of woe
That we have borne for thee.
Thus may we consolation tear
E'en from the depth of our despair
And wasting misery.

The nightly anguish thou art spared
When all the crushing truth is bared
To the awakening mind,
When the galled heart is pierced with grief,
Till wildly it implores relief,
But small relief can find.

Nor know'st thou what it is to lie
Looking forth with streaming eye
On life's lone wilderness.
'Weary, weary, dark and drear,
How shall I the journey bear,
The burden and distress?'

Then since thou art spared such pain
We shall not wish thee here again;
He that lives must mourn
God help us through our misery
And give us rest and joy with thee
When we reach our bourne!

EMILY BRONTË (1818-1848)

By far the finest poet of her talented family, Emily Brontë's life was cut short by tuberculosis, the disease that killed three of her four sisters. Many of her poems, notably her last, 'No Coward's Soul is Mine', show her courageously facing the prospect of her own death.

THE PHILOSOPHER

Enough of thought, philosopher!
Too long hast thou been dreaming
Unlightened in this chamber drear
While summer's sun is beaming!
Space-sweeping soul, what sad refrain
Concludes thy musings once again?
'Oh, for the time when I shall sleep
Without identity,
And never care how rain may steep,
Or snow may cover me!
No promised heaven, these wild desires
Could all, or half fulfil;
No threatened hell, with quenchless fires,
Subdue this quenchless will!'

'So said I, and still say the same;
Still, to my death, will say
Three gods, within this little frame,

Are warring, night and day;
Heaven could not hold them all, and yet
They all are held in me;
And must be mine till I forget
My present entity!
Oh, for the time, when in my breast
Their struggles will be o'er!
Oh, for the day, when I shall rest,
And never suffer more!'

'I saw a spirit, standing, man,
Where thou dost stand – an hour ago,
And round his feet three rivers ran,
Of equal depth, and equal flow –
A golden stream – and one like blood;
And one like sapphire seemed to be;
But where they joined their triple flood
It tumbled in an inky sea.
The spirit sent his dazzling gaze
Down through that ocean's gloomy night;
Then, kindling all, with sudden blaze,
The glad deep sparkled wide and bright –
White as the sun, far, far more fair
Than its divided sources were!'

'And even for that spirit, seer,
I've watched and sought my lifetime long;
Sought him in heaven, hell, earth, and air,
An endless search, and always wrong.
Had I but seen his glorious eye

Once light the clouds that 'wilder me,
I ne'er had raised this coward cry
To cease to think, and cease to be;
I ne'er had called oblivion blest,
Nor, stretching eager hands to death,
Implored to change for senseless rest
This sentient soul, this living breath.
Oh, let me die – that power and will
Their cruel strife may close;
And conquered good and conquering ill
Be lost in one repose!'

DEATH

Death! that struck when I was most confiding
In my certain faith of joy to be
Strike again, Time's withered branch dividing
From the fresh root of Eternity!

Leaves, upon Time's branch, were growing brightly,
Full of sap, and full of silver-dew;
Birds beneath its shelter gathered nightly;
Daily round its flowers the wild bees flew.

Sorrow passed, and plucked the golden blossom;
Guilt stripped off the foliage in its pride;
But, within its parent's kindly bosom,
Flowed for ever Life's restoring tide.

Little mourned I for the parted gladness,
For the vacant nest and silent song
Hope was there, and laughed me out of sadness,
Whispering, 'Winter will not linger long!'

And, behold! with tenfold increase blessing,
Spring adorned the beauty-burdened spray;
Wind and rain and fervent heat, caressing,
Lavished glory on that second May!

High it rose – no wingèd grief could sweep it;
Sin was scared to distance with its shine;
Love, and its own life, had power to keep it
From all wrong – from every blight but thine!

Cruel Death! The young leaves droop and languish
Evening's gentle air may still restore –
No! the morning sunshine mocks my anguish
Time, for me, must never blossom more!

Strike it down, that other boughs may flourish
Where that perished sapling used to be;
Thus, at least, its mouldering corpse will nourish
That from which It sprung – Eternity.

'ALL DAY I'VE TOILED BUT NOT WITH PAIN'

All day I've toiled, but not with pain,
In learning's golden mine;

And now at eventide again
The moonbeams softly shine.

There is no snow upon the ground,
No frost on wind or wave;
The south wind blew with gentlest sound
And broke their icy grave.

'Tis sweet to wander here at night
To watch the winter die,
With heart as summer sunshine light
And warm as summer sky.

O may I never lose the peace
That lulls me gently now,
Though time should change my youthful face,
And years should shade my brow!

True to myself, and true to all,
May I be healthful still,
And turn away from passion's call,
And curb my own wild will.

'RICHES I HOLD IN LIGHT ESTEEM'

Riches I hold in light esteem
And Love I laugh to scorn
And lust of Fame was but a dream
That vanished with the morn

And if l pray, the only prayer
That moves my lips for me
Is – 'Leave the heart that now I bear
And give me liberty.'

'NO COWARD SOUL IS MINE'

No coward soul is mine,
No trembler in the world's storm-troubled sphere.
I see Heaven's glories shine
And Faith stands equal arming me from Fear.

O God within my breast,
Almighty ever-present Deity,
Life, that in me hast rest
As I, Undying Life, have power in Thee.

Vain are the thousand creeds
That move men's hearts, unutterably vain,
Worthless as withered weeds
Or idlest froth amid the boundless main.

To waken doubt in one
Holding so fast by thy infinity,
So surely anchored on
The steadfast rock of Immortality.

With wide-embracing love
Thy spirit animates eternal years,

Pervades and broods above,

Changes, sustains, dissolves, creates and rears.

Though Earth and moon were gone

And suns and universes ceased to be

And thou wert left alone

Every Existence would exist in thee.

There is not room for Death

Nor atom that his might could render void

Since thou art Being and Breath

And what thou art may never be destroyed.

GEORGE ELIOT (1819-1880)

The novels of George Eliot – born Mary Ann Evans in an era when novel-writing was not a respectable profession for a woman – have gone in and out of fashion, though many people consider Middlemarch *the perfect example of the form and Virginia Woolf described it as 'one of the few English novels written for grown-up people'. Her poetry has never been widely read, but these opening lines of a much longer poem show the same combination of pathos and humour that characterise her more famous works.*

A MINOR PROPHET (extract)

I have a friend, a vegetarian seer,

By name Elias Baptist Butterworth,

A harmless, bland, disinterested man,

Whose ancestors in Cromwell's day believed

The Second Advent certain in five years,

But when King Charles the Second came instead,

Revised their date and sought another world:

I mean – not heaven but – America.

A fervid stock, whose generous hope embraced

The fortunes of mankind, not stopping short

At rise of leather, or the fall of gold,

Nor listening to the voices of the time

As housewives listen to a cackling hen,

With wonder whether she has laid her egg

On their own nest-egg. Still they did insist –

Somewhat too wearisomely on the joys

Of their Millennium, when coats and hats

Would all be of one pattern, books and songs

All fit for Sundays, and the casual talk

As good as sermons preached extempore.

And in Elias the ancestral zeal

Breathes strong as ever, only modified

By Transatlantic air and modern thought.

You could not pass him in the street and fail

To note his shoulders' long declivity,

Beard to the waist, swan-neck, and large pale eyes;

Or, when he lifts his hat, to mark his hair

Brushed back to show his great capacity –

A full grain's length at the angle of the brow

Proving him witty, while the shallower men

Only seem witty in their repartees.

Not that he's vain, but that his doctrine needs

FEEDING THE CHICKENS BY ERNEST WALBOURN, FLOURISHED 1897-1904.

The testimony of his frontal lobe.
On all points he adopts the latest views;
Takes for the key of universal Mind...

And when all Earth is vegetarian –
When, lacking butchers, quadrupeds die out,
And less Thought-atmosphere is reabsorbed
By nerves of insects parasitical,
Those higher truths, seized now by higher minds
But not expressed (the insects hindering)
Will either flash out into eloquence,
Or better still, be comprehensible
By rappings simply, without need of roots.

'Tis on this theme the vegetarian world –
That good Elias willingly expands:
He loves to tell in mildly nasal tones
And vowels stretched to suit the widest views,
The future fortunes of our infant Earth –
When it will be too full of human kind
To have the room for wilder animals.
Saith he, Sahara will be populous
With families of gentlemen retired
From commerce in more Central Africa,
Who order coolness as we order coal,
And have a lobe anterior strong enough
To think away the sand-storms. Science thus
Will leave no spot on this terraqueous globe
Unfit to be inhabited by man,
The chief of animals: all meaner brutes

Will have been smoked and elbowed out of life.

No lions then shall lap Caffrarian pools,

Or shake the Atlas with their midnight roar:

Even the slow, slime-loving crocodile,

The last of animals to take a hint,

Will then retire for ever from a scene

Where public feeling strongly sets against him.

Fishes may lead carnivorous lives obscure,

But must not dream of culinary rank

Or being dished in good society.

Imagination in that distant age,

Aiming at fiction called historical,

Will vainly try to reconstruct the times

When it was men's preposterous delight

To sit astride live horses, which consumed

Materials for incalculable cakes;

When there were milkmaids who drew milk from cows

With udders kept abnormal for that end...

'Tis to be feared, though, that the duller boys,

Much given to anachronisms and nuts,

(Elias has confessed boys will be boys)

May write a jockey for a centaur, think

Europa's suitor was an Irish bull,

Aesop a journalist who wrote up Fox,

And Bruin a chief swindler upon 'Change.

Boys will be boys, but dogs will all be moral,

With longer alimentary canals

Suited to diet vegetarian.

The uglier breeds will fade from memory,

Or, being palaeontological,

Live but as portraits in large learned books,

Distasteful to the feelings of an age

Nourished on purest beauty. Earth will hold

No stupid brutes, no cheerful queernesses,

No naive cunning, grave absurdity.

Wart-pigs with tender and parental grunts,

Wombats much flattened as to their contour,

Perhaps from too much crushing in the ark,

But taking meekly that fatality;

The serious cranes, unstung by ridicule;

Long-headed, short-legged, solemn-looking curs,

(Wise, silent critics of a flippant age);

The silly straddling foals, the weak-brained geese

Hissing fallaciously at sound of wheels –

All these rude products will have disappeared

Along with every faulty human type.

By dint of diet vegetarian

All will be harmony of hue and line,

Bodies and minds all perfect, limbs well-turned,

And talk quite free from aught erroneous.

JULIA WARD HOWE (1819-1910)

Julia Ward Howe is best known for 'The Battle Hymn of the Republic', which she wrote in great excitement on her return from visiting an army camp during the American Civil War. Born into wealthy New York society, she chose to live a less glamorous life, campaigning for worthy causes, notably the abolition of slavery.

THE BATTLE HYMN OF THE REPUBLIC

Mine eyes have seen the glory of the coming of the Lord:
He is trampling out the vintage where the grapes of wrath are stored;
He hath loosed the fateful lightning of His terrible swift sword:
His truth is marching on.

I have seen Him in the watch fires of a hundred circling camps;
They have builded Him an altar in the evening dews and damps;
I can read His righteous sentence by the dim and flaring lamps.
His day is marching on.

I have read a fiery gospel writ in burnished rows of steel:
'As ye deal with my contemners so my grace with you will deal';
Let the Hero, born of woman, crush the serpent with His heel,
Since God is marching on.

He has sounded forth the trumpet that shall never call retreat;
He is sifting out the hearts of men before His judgement seat:
Oh! be swift, my soul, to answer Him! be jubilant, my feet!
Our God is marching on.

In the beauty of the lilies Christ was born across the sea,
With a glory in His bosom that transfigures you and me:
As He died to make men holy, let us die to make men free,
While God is marching on.

❦

OUR ORDERS

Weave no more silks, ye Lyons looms,
To deck our girls for gay delights!
The crimson flower of battle blooms,
And solemn marches fill the night.

Weave but the flag whose bars to-day
Drooped heavy o'er our early dead,
And homely garments, coarse and grey,
For orphans that must earn their bread!

Keep back your tunes, ye viols sweet,
That poured delight from other lands!
Rouse there the dancer's restless feet:
The trumpet leads our warrior bands.

And ye that wage the war of words
With mystic fame and subtle power,
Go, chatter to the idle birds,
Or teach the lesson of the hour!...

And if that destiny could fail,
The sun should darken in the sky,
The eternal bloom of Nature pale,
And God, and Truth, and Freedom die!

ஃ

Cecil Frances Alexander (?1820-1895)

Born in Strabane, in what is now Northern Ireland, Cecil Alexander was married to the Archbishop of Armagh and is best known for her Hymns for Little Children *– she is the author, among many others, of 'Once in Royal David's City' and 'All Things Bright and Beautiful'.*

Dreams

Beyond, beyond the mountain line,
The grey-stone and the boulder,
Beyond the growth of dark green pine,
That crowns its western shoulder,
There lies that fairy-land of mine,
Unseen of a beholder.

Its fruits are all like rubies rare;
Its streams are clear as glasses;
There golden castles hang in air,
And purple grapes in masses,
And noble knights and ladies fair
Come riding down the passes.

Ah me! they say if I could stand
Upon those mountain ledges,
I should but see on either hand
Plain fields and dusty hedges;
And yet I know my fairy-land
Lies somewhere o'er their edges.

WOMEN'S POETRY

ANNE BRONTË (1820-1849)

Much of Anne Brontë's poetry is overshadowed with a gloom which can be attributed partly to the sorrows of her short life – although she died before she was thirty, she outlived all but one of her five siblings – and partly to her unwillingness to believe in a God who could bring such misery on beings of his own creation. She came to believe that she was not one of God's chosen, and found the injustice of this hard to accept.

THE ARBOUR

I'll rest me in this sheltered bower,
And look upon the clear blue sky
That smiles upon me through the trees,
Which stand so thickly clustering by;

And view their green and glossy leaves,
All glistening in the sunshine fair,
And list the rustling of their boughs,
So softly whispering through the air.

And while my ear drinks in the sound,
My wingèd soul shall fly away;
Reviewing long departed years
As one mild, beaming, autumn day;

And soaring on to future scenes,
Like hills and woods, and valleys green,
All basking in the summer's sun,
But distant still, and dimly seen.

Oh, list! 'tis summer's very breath
That gently shakes the rustling trees –
But look! the snow is on the ground –
How can I think of scenes like these?

'Tis but the *frost* that clears the air,
And gives the sky that lovely blue;
They're smiling in a *winter's* sun,
Those evergreens of sombre hue.

And winter's chill is on my heart –
How can I dream of future bliss?
How can my spirit soar away,
Confined by such a chain as this?

IF THIS BE ALL

O God! if this indeed be all
That Life can show to me;
If on my aching brow may fall
No freshening dew from Thee,

If with no brighter light than this
The lamp of hope may glow,
And I may only dream of bliss,
And wake to weary woe;

If friendship's solace must decay,
When other joys are gone,

And love must keep so far away,
While I go wandering on,

Wandering and toiling without gain,
The slave of others' will,
With constant care and frequent pain,
Despised, forgotten still;

Grieving to look on vice and sin,
Yet powerless to quell
The silent current from within,
The outward torrent's swell;

While all the good I would impart,
The feelings I would share,
Are driven backward to my heart,
And turned to wormwood there;

If clouds must ever keep from sight
The glories of the Sun,
And I must suffer Winter's blight,
Ere Summer is begun:

If Life must be so full of care,
Then call me soon to Thee;
Or give me strength enough to bear
My load of misery.

OPPOSITE. THE PASS OF KILLIECRANKIE BY HARRY SUTTON PALMER.

LADY WILDE ('Speranza') (c. 1820-1896)

Lady Wilde – born Jane Elgee in County Wexford, Ireland – is best known as the mother of Oscar, but she achieved wide recognition for her own poetry and prose, especially that published in the newspaper The Nation *under the pseudonym 'Speranza'. She would have been in her late twenties during the great potato famine, when Irish resentment against the ruling English was at its height.*

THE FAMINE YEAR

Weary men, what reap ye? – 'Golden corn for the stranger.'
What sow ye? – 'Human corses that wait for the avenger.'
Fainting forms, hunger-stricken, what see ye in the offing?
'Stately ships to bear our food away amid the stranger's scoffing
There's a proud array of soldiers – what do they round your door?
'They guard our master's granaries from the thin hands of the poor.'
Pale mothers, wherefore weeping? 'Would to God that we were dead –
Our children swoon before us, – and we cannot give them bread!'

Little children, tears are strange upon your infant faces,
God meant you but to smile within your mother's soft embraces.
'Oh! we know not what is smiling, and we know not what is dying;
But we're hungry, very hungry, and we cannot stop our crying.
And some of us grow cold and white – we know not what it means;
But as they lie beside us we tremble in our dreams.'
There's a gaunt crowd on the highway – are you come to pray to man,
With hollow eyes that cannot weep, and for words your faces wan?

OPPOSITE. THE OLD CLOCK TOWER, YOUGHAL, BY ALEXANDER WILLIAMS, 1846-1930.

'No; the blood is dead within our veins – we care not now for life;

Let us die hid in the ditches, far from children and from wife!

We cannot stay to listen to their raving famished cries –

Bread! Bread! Bread! and none to still their agonies.

We left an infant playing with her dead mother's hand:

We left a maiden maddened by the fever's scorching brand.'

Better, maiden, thou wert strangled in thy own dark-twisted tresses!

Better, infant, thou wert smothered in thy mother's first caresses.

'We are fainting in our misery, but God will hear our groan;

Yet, if fellow-men desert us, will He hearken from His throne?

Accursed are we in our own land, yet toil we still and toil;

But the stranger reaps our harvest – the alien owns our soil.

O Christ! how have we sinned, that on our native plains

We perish homeless, naked, starved, with branded brow like Cain's?

Dying, dying wearily, with a torture sure and slow –

Dying as a dog would die, by the wayside as we go.

'One by one they're falling round us, their pale faces to the sky

We've no strength left to dig them graves — there let them lie,

The wild bird, if he's stricken, is mourned by the others,

But we – we die in Christian land, – we die amid our brothers,

In the land which God has given, like a wild beast in his cave,

Without a tear, a prayer, a shroud, a coffin, or a grave.

Ha! but think ye the contortions on each livid face ye see,

Will not be read on Judgement Day by eyes of Deity?

'We are wretches, famished, scorned, human tools to build your pride,

But God will yet take vengeance for the souls for whom Christ died.

Now is your hour of pleasure – bask ye in the world's caress;
But our whitening bones against ye will rise as witnesses,
From the cabins and the ditches in their charred, uncoffined masses,
For the Angel of the Trumpet will know them as he passes.
A ghastly spectral army, before great God we'll stand,
And arraign ye as our murderers, O spoilers of our land!'

THE EXODUS (extract)

'A million a decade!' Calmly and cold
The units are read by our statesmen sage;
Little they think of a Nation old,
Fading away from History's page;
Outcast weeds by a desolate sea –
Fallen leaves of Humanity.

'A million a decade!' – of human wrecks,
Corpses lying in fever sheds –
Corpses huddled on foundering decks,
And shroudless dead on their rocky beds;
Nerve and muscle, and heart and brain,
Lost to Ireland – lost in vain

'A million a decade!' Count ten by ten,
Column and line of the record fair;
Each unit stands for ten thousand men,
Staring with blank, dead eye-balls there;
Strewn like blasted trees on the sod,
Men that were made in the image of God.

'A million a decade!' – and nothing done;
The Caesars had less to conquer a world;
The war for the Right not yet begun,
The banner of Freedom not yet unfurled:
The soil is fed by the weed that dies;
If forest leaves fall, yet they fertilise.

But ye – dead, dead, not climbing the height,
Not clearing a path for the future to tread;
Not opening the golden portals of light,
Ere the gate was choked by your piled-up dead:
Martyrs ye, yet never a name
Shines on the golden roll of Fame....

'A million a decade!' What does it mean?
A Nation dying of inner decay –
A churchyard silence where life has been –
The base of the pyramid crumbling away:
A drift of men gone over the sea,
A drift of the dead where men should be.

Was it for this ye plighted your word,
Crowned and crownless rulers of men?
Have ye kept faith with your crucified Lord,
And fed His sheep till He comes again?
Or fled like hireling shepherds away,
Leaving the fold the gaunt wolf's prey?...

Ye stand at the Judgment-bar to-day –
The Angels are counting the dead-roll, too;

Have ye trod in the pure and perfect way,
And ruled for God as the crowned should do?
Count our dead – before angels and men,
Ye're judged and doomed by the Statist's pen.

ADELAIDE ANNE PROCTER (1825–1864)

Adelaide Procter's mother ran a literary 'salon' frequented by Dickens and Thackeray.
Adelaide submitted her first poems to Dickens' journal Household Words *under a*
pseudonym and had the satisfaction of seeing them accepted on their own merits. She became
extremely successful, although some of her poetry may be too sentimental for modern taste.

HOMELESS

It is cold dark midnight, yet listen
To that patter of tiny feet!
Is it one of your dogs, fair lady,
Who whines in the bleak cold street?
Is it one of your silken spaniels
Shut out in the snow and the sleet?

My dogs sleep warm in their baskets,
Safe from the darkness and snow;
All the beasts in our Christian England,
Find pity wherever they go –
(Those are only the homeless children
Who are wandering to and fro.)

Look out in the gusty darkness –
I have seen it again and again,
That shadow, that flits so slowly
Up and down past the window pane: –
It is surely some criminal lurking
Out there in the frozen rain?

Nay, our Criminals all are sheltered,
They are pitied and taught and fed:
That is only a sister-woman
Who has got neither food nor bed –
And the Night cries 'sin to be living',
And the River cries 'sin to be dead'.

Look out at that farthest corner
Where the wall stands blank and bare: –
Can that be a pack which a Pedlar
Has left and forgotten there?
His goods lying out unsheltered
Will be spoilt by the damp night air.

Nay; – goods in our thrifty England
Are not left to lie and grow rotten,
For each man knows the market value
Of silk or woollen or cotton...
But in counting the riches of England
I think our Poor are forgotten.

OPPOSITE. WOODLAND LANDSCAPE IN WINTER BY JAMES THOMAS WATTS, 1853-1930.

Our Beasts and our Thieves and our Chattels
Have weight for good or for ill;
But the Poor are only His image,
His presence, His word, His will –
And so Lazarus lies at our doorstep
And Dives neglects him still.

FRANCES W. HARPER (1825-1911)

Frances Harper, born in Baltimore, Maryland, to free black parents, was one of the most prominent anti-slavery activists of her day. She was also a popular poet and has the distinction of being the first black American woman to have a novel published.

SHE'S FREE

How say that by law we may torture and chase
A woman whose crime is the hue of her face? –
With her step on the ice, and her arm on her child,
The danger was fearful, the pathway was wild…
But she's free! yes, free from the land where the slave
From the hand of oppression must rest in the grave;
Where bondage and blood, where scourges and chains,
Have placed on their banner indelible stains…
The bloodhounds have miss'd the scent of her way,
The hunter is rifled and foiled of his prey,
The cursing of men and clanking of chains
Make sounds of strange discord on Liberty's plains…

Oh! poverty, danger and death she can brave
For the child of her love is no longer a slave.

EMILY PFEIFFER (1827-1890)

When a Times *review of Emily Pfeiffer's work suggested that no woman was worthy of the name of poet, she responded on what she described as 'a topic of much wider interest', deploring 'the tyranny of circumstances' that had held women back in so many fields. Her poetry and essays alike advocated women's right to go into professional employment, and to be granted the vote.*

THE WINGED SOUL

My soul is like some cage-born bird, that hath
A restless prescience – howsoever won –
Of a broad pathway leading to the sun,
With promptings of an oft-reprovèd faith
In sun-ward yearnings. Stricken though her breast,
And faint her wing with beating at the bars
Of sense, she looks beyond outlying stars,
And only in the Infinite sees rest.

Sad soul! If ever thy desire be bent.
Or broken to thy doom, and made to share
The ruminant's beatitude – content
Chewing the cud of knowledge, with no care
For germs of life within; then will I say,
Thou art not caged, but fitly stalled in clay!

CHRISTINA ROSSETTI (1830-1894)

Sister of the Pre-Raphaelite painter Dante Gabriel Rossetti, Christina Rossetti produced a large quantity of poetry and prose whose characteristic melancholy may have been the result of chronic ill-health and an unhappy love affair.

MY SECRET

I tell my secret? No indeed, not I:
Perhaps some day, who knows?
But not today; it froze, and blows, and snows,
And you're too curious: fie!
You want to hear it? well:
Only, my secret's mine, and I won't tell.

Or, after all, perhaps there's none:
Suppose there is no secret after all,
But only just my fun.
Today's a nipping day, a biting day;
In which one wants a shawl,
A veil, a cloak, and other wraps:
I cannot ope to every one who taps,
And let the draughts come whistling thro' my hall;
Come bounding and surrounding me,
Come buffeting, astounding me,
Nipping and clipping thro' my wraps and all.
I wear my mask for warmth: who ever shows
His nose to Russian snows
To be pecked at by every wind that blows?

You would not peck? I thank you for good will,
Believe, but leave that truth untested still.

Spring's an expansive time: yet I don't trust
March with its peck of dust,
Nor April with its rainbow-crowned brief showers,
Nor even May, whose flowers
One frost may wither thro' the sunless hours.

Perhaps some languid summer day,
When drowsy birds sing less and less,
And golden fruit is ripening to excess,
If there's not too much sun nor too much cloud,
And the warm wind is neither still nor loud,
Perhaps my secret I may say,
Or you may guess.

Up-Hill

Does the road wind up-hill all the way?
Yes, to the very end.
Will the day's journey take the whole long day?
From morn to night, my friend.

But is there for the night a resting-place?
A roof for when the slow dark hours begin.
May not the darkness hide it from my face?
You cannot miss that inn.

Shall I meet other wayfarers at night?

Those who have gone before.

Then must I knock, or call when just in sight?

They will not keep you standing at that door.

Shall I find comfort, travel-sore and weak?

Of labour you shall find the sum.

Will there be beds for me and all who seek?

Yea, beds for all who come.

REMEMBER

Remember me when I am gone away,

Gone far away into the silent land;

When you can no more hold me by

Nor I half turn to go yet turning stay.

Remember me when no more day by day

You tell me of our future that you planned:

Only remember me; you understand

It will be late to counsel then or pray.

Yet if you should forget me for a while

And afterwards remember, do not grieve:

For if the darkness and corruption leave

A vestige of the thoughts that once I had,

Better by far you should forget and smile

Than that you should remember and be sad.

OPPOSITE. A STUDY FOR DAYDREAM BY DANTE GABRIEL ROSSETTI, 1828-1882.

EMILY DICKINSON (1830-1886)

Emily Dickinson lived a quiet, almost reclusive life in her father's home in Amherst, Massachusetts, and refused to let much of her poetry be published in her lifetime. Although some of her early work suggests an unhappy or unrequited love affair, her later poems are more mystical, showing a deep love of God and a fascination with death.

'I LOST A WORLD – THE OTHER DAY!'

I lost a World – the other day!
Has Anybody found?
You'll know it by the Row of Stars
Around its forehead bound

A Rich man – might not notice it –
Yet – to my frugal Eye,
Of more Esteem than Ducats –
Oh find it – Sir – for me!

'BECAUSE I COULD NOT STOP FOR DEATH'

Because I could not stop for Death –
He kindly stopped for me –
The Carriage held but just Ourselves –
And Immortality.

We slowly drove – He knew no haste
And I had put away . . .

My labor and my leisure too,
For His Civility –

We passed the School, where Children strove
At Recess – in the Ring –
We passed the Fields of Gazing Grain –
We passed the Setting Sun –

Or rather – He passed Us –
The Dews drew quivering and chill –
For only Gossamer, my Gown –
My Tippet – only Tulle –

We paused before a House that seemed
A Swelling of the Ground –
The Roof was scarcely visible
The Cornice – in the Ground –

Since then – 'tis Centuries – and yet
Feels shorter than the Day
I first surmised the Horses' Heads
Were toward Eternity.

'HAD I KNOWN THAT THE FIRST WAS THE LAST'

Had I known that the first was the last
I should have kept it longer.
Had I known that the last was the first

I should have drunk it stronger.

Cup, it was your fault,

Lip was not the liar.

No, lip, it was yours,

Bliss was most to blame.

'HE WAS MY HOST – HE WAS MY GUEST'

He was my host – he was my guest,

I never to this day

If I invited him could tell,

Or he invited me.

So infinite our intercourse

So intimate, indeed,

Analysis as capsule seemed

To keeper of the seed

SUSAN COOLIDGE (1835-1905)

The author of the children's classic What Katy Did *and its sequels was noted for the lack
of sentimentality which characterised her work and set it apart
from many contemporary writers for children. The same praise could be
given to the cheery little poem on page 92.*

OPPOSITE. GIRL WITH A SLATE BY L. M. WATSON, FLOURISHED NINETEENTH CENTURY.

NEW EVERY MORNING

Every day is a fresh beginning,
Listen my soul to the glad refrain.
And, spite of old sorrows
And older sinning,
Troubles forecasted
And possible pain,
Take heart with the day and begin again.

ADA CAMBRIDGE (1844-1926)

Born in Norfolk, Ada Cambridge emigrated at the age of twenty-six to Australia, where her husband was to be a missionary priest. Although her ideas are inevitably coloured by the conventions of her time, her writing frequently called upon women to think for themselves.

HONOUR

Me let the world disparage and despise –
The world, that hugs its soul-corroding chains,
The world, that spends for such ignoble gains.
Let foe or bigot wrap my name in lies;
Let Justice, blind and maimed and halt, chastise
The rebel-spirit surging in my veins;
Let the Law deal me penalties and pains;
Let me be outcast in my neighbours' eyes.

But let me fall not in my own esteem,

By poor deceit or petty greed debased;

Let me be clean from undetected shame;

Know myself true, though heretic I seem;

Know myself faithful, howsoe'er disgraced;

Upright and strong, for all the load of blame.

EMILY HENRIETTA HICKEY (1845-1924)

Emily Hickey was a prolific Irish poet, one of the founders of the Browning Society. This verse seems to echo some of Browning's work.

BELOVED IT IS MORN

Beloved, it is morn!

A redder berry on the thorn,

A deeper yellow on the corn,

For this good day new-born.

Pray, Sweet, for me

That I may be

Faithful to God and thee.

Beloved, it is day!

And lovers work, as children play,

With heart and brain untired alway:

Dear love, look up and pray.

Pray, Sweet, for me

That I may be
Faithful to God and thee.
Beloved, it is night!
Thy heart and mine are full of light,
Thy spirit shineth clear and white,
God keep thee in His sight!
Pray, Sweet, for me
That I may be
Faithful to God and thee.

EMILY LAWLESS (1845-1913)

The daughter of an Irish peer, Emily Lawless was one of many women poets of the nineteenth century who came from privileged backgrounds, were well educated and well travelled, never married, and wrote extensively and intelligently. Her works include poems, novels and a history of Ireland.

DIRGE OF THE MUNSTER FOREST (1591)

Bring out the hemlock! bring the funeral yew!
The faithful ivy that doth all enfold;
Heap high the rocks, the patient brown earth strew,
And cover them against the numbing cold.
Marshal my retinue of bird and beast,
Wren, titmouse, robin, birds of every hue;
Let none keep back, no, not the very least,
Nor fox, nor deer, nor tiny nibbling crew,

Only bid one of all my forest clan

Keep far from us on this our funeral day.

On the grey wolf I lay my sovereign ban,

The great grey wolf who scrapes the earth away;

Lest, with hooked claw and furious hunger, he

Lay bare my dead for gloating foes to see –

Lay bare my dead, who died, and died for me.

For I must surely die as they have died,

And lo! my doom stands yoked and linked with theirs;

The axe is sharpened to cut down my pride:

I pass, I die, and leave no natural heirs,

THE GAP OF DUNLOE, KILLARNEY.

Soon shall my sylvan coronals be cast;

My hidden sanctuaries, my secret ways,

Naked must stand to the rebellious blast;

No Spring shall quicken what this Autumn slays.

Therefore, while still I keep my russet crown,

I summon all my lieges to the feast.

Hither, ye flutterers! black, or pied, or brown;

Hither, ye furred ones! Hither every beast!

Only to one of all my forest clan I cry,

'Avaunt! Our mourning revels flee!'

On the grey wolf I lay my sovereign ban,

The great grey wolf with scraping claws, lest he

Lay bare my dead for gloating foes to see –

Lay bare my dead, who died, and died for me.

ALICE MEYNELL (1847-1922)

*A prolific poet and essayist, Alice Meynell was twice nominated as a possible Poet
Laureate. She converted to Catholicismwhile still in her teens and followed its teachings
faithfully in her life and work. She married the author and editor Wilfrid Meynell – who
had initially been attracted by her poetry – and moved in distinguished
Catholic and literary circles.*

A LETTER FROM A GIRL TO HER OWN OLD AGE

Listen, and when thy hand this paper presses,

O time-worn woman, think of her who blesses

What thy thin fingers touch, with her caresses.

O mother, for a weight of years do break thee!
O daughter, for slow time must yet awake thee,
And from the changes of my heart must make thee.

O fainting traveller, morn is grey in heaven.
Dost thou remember how the clouds were driven?
And are they calm about the fall of even?

Pause near the ending of thy long migration,
For this one sudden hour of desolation
Appeals to one hour of thy meditation.

Suffer, O silent one, that I remind thee
Of the great hills that storm the sky behind thee,
Of the wild winds of power that have resigned thee.

Know that the mournful plain where thou must wander,
Is but a grey and silent world, but ponder
The misty mountains of the morning yonder.

Listen; the mountain winds with rain were fretting,
And sudden gleams the mountain-tops besetting.
I cannot let thee fade to death, forgetting.

What part of this wild heart of mine I know not
Will follow with thee where the great winds blow not,
And where the young flowers of the mountain grow not.

Yet let my letter with thy lost thoughts in it
Tell what the way was when thou didst begin it,
And win with thee the goal when thou shalt win it.

Oh, in some hour of thine my thoughts shall guide thee.
Suddenly, though time, darkness, silence hide thee,
This wind from thy lost country flits beside thee;

Telling thee: all thy memories moved the maiden,
With thy regrets was morning over-shaden,
With sorrow thou hast left, her life was laden.

But whither shall my thoughts turn to pursue thee?
Life changes, and the years and days renew thee.
Oh, Nature brings my straying heart unto thee.

Her winds will join us, with their constant kisses
Upon the evening as the morning tresses,
Her summers breathe the same unchanging blisses.

And we, so altered in our shifting phases,
Track one another 'mid the many mazes
By the eternal child-breath of the daisies.

I have not writ this letter of divining
To make a glory of thy silent pining.
A triumph of thy mute and strange declining.

Only one youth, and the bright life was shrouded.
Only one morning, and the day was clouded.

And one old age with all regrets is crowded.

Oh, hush; oh, hush! Thy tears my words are steeping.
Oh, hush, hush, hush! So full, the fount of weeping?
Poor eyes, so quickly moved, so near to sleeping?

Pardon the girl; such strange desires beset her.
Poor woman, lay aside the mournful letter
That breaks thy heart; the one that wrote, forget her.

The one that now thy faded features guesses,
With filial fingers thy grey hair caresses,
With morning tears thy mournful twilight blesses.

EMMA LAZARUS (1849-1887)

Born into a New York Sephardic Jewish family, Emma Lazarus worked among Russian Jewish refugees on Ellis Island, the first landfall for all would-be immigrants. The stories she heard there of the pogroms in Russia made her an early advocate for the creation of a Jewish homeland, and a passionate defender of the rights of Jews to view the United States as a refuge. Her best-known poem, 'The New Colossus', was written in honour of the Statue of Liberty and engraved on a plaque fixed to its base in 1903.

THE NEW COLOSSUS

Not like the brazen giant of Greek fame,
With conquering limbs astride from land to land;
Here at our sea-washed, sunset gates shall stand
A mighty woman with a torch, whose flame

Is the imprisoned lightning, and her name
Mother of Exiles. From her beacon-hand
Glows world-wide welcome; her mild eyes command
The air-bridged harbor that twin cities frame.
'Keep, ancient lands, your storied pomp!' cries she
With silent lips. 'Give me your tired, your poor,
Your huddled masses yearning to breathe free,
The wretched refuse of your teeming shore.
Send these, the homeless, tempest-tost to me,
I lift my lamp beside the golden door!'

THE BANNER OF THE JEW

Wake, Israel, wake! Recall today
The glorious Maccabean rage,
The sire heroic, hoary-grey,
His five-fold lion-lineage:
The Wise, the Elect, the Help-of-God,
The Burst-of-Spring, the Avenging Rod.

From Mizpeh's mountain-ridge they saw
Jerusalem's empty streets, her shrine
Laid waste where Greeks profaned the Law,
With idol and with pagan sign.
Mourners in tattered black were there,
With ashes sprinkled on their hair.

Then from the stony peak there rang
A blast to ope the graves; down poured

The Maccabean clan, who sang
Their battle-anthem to the Lord.
Five heroes lead, and following, see,
Ten thousand rush to Victory!

THE 'HUDDLED MASSES' OF IMMIGRANTS OFTEN CAME FROM THE POVERTY-STRICKEN
SHORES OF IRELAND. IN THE EARLY 1900S THE ARTIST FRANCIS WALKER RECORDED THIS
SCENE OF FAMILIES AT KILLARNEY RAILWAY STATION, SAYING GOODBYE TO
LOVED ONES BOUND FOR AMERICA.

Oh for Jerusalem's trumpet now,
To blow a blast of shattering power,
To wake the sleepers high and low,
And rouse them to the urgent hour!
No hand for vengeance – but to save,
A million naked swords should wave.

Oh deem not dead that martial fire,
Say not the mystic flame is spent!
With Moses' law and David's lyre,
Your ancient strength remains unbent.
Let but an Ezra rise anew
To lift the Banner of the Jew.

A rag, a mock at first – erelong,
When men have bled, and women wept
To guard its precious folds from wrong,
Even they who shrunk, even they who slept,
Shall leap to bless it, and to save.
Strike! for the brave revere the brave!

❧❧❧

ISABELLA VALANCY CRAWFORD (1850-1887)

Born in Dublin, Isabella Crawford emigrated with her family to Canada as a child of
eight and lived in various small towns, where she must have observed
the pioneering life that inspired this poem.

THE CANOE

My masters twain made me a bed
Of pine-boughs resinous, and cedar;
Of moss, a soft and gentle breeder
Of dreams of rest; and me they spread
With furry skins, and, laughing, said –
'Now she shall lay her polished sides
As queens do rest, or dainty brides,
Our slender lady of the tides!'

My masters twain their camp-soul lit,
Streamed incense from the hissing cones;
Large crimson flashes grew and whirled,
Thin golden nerves of sly light curled,
Round the dun camp, and rose faint zones
Half-way about each grim bole knit,
Like a shy child that would bedeck
With its soft clasp a Brave's red neck,
Yet sees the rough shield on his breast,
The awful plumes shake on his crest,
And fearful drops his timid face,
Nor dares complete the sweet embrace.

Into the hollow hearts of brakes
Yet warm from sides of does and stags,
Passed to the crisp dark river flags,
Sinous, red as copper, snakes –
Sharp-headed serpents, made of light,
Glided and hid themselves in night.

My masters twain the slaughtered deer
Hung on forked boughs, with thongs of leather.
Bound were his stiff, slim feet together,
His eyes like dead stars cold and drear;
The wandering firelight drew near
And laid its wide palm, red and anxious,
On the sharp splendor of his branches;
On the white foam grown hard and sere
On flank and shoulder.
Death, hard as breast of granite boulder,
And under his lashes,
Peered through his eyes at his life's gray ashes.

My masters twain sang songs that wove
(As they burnished hunting blade and rifle)
A golden thread with a cobweb trifle,
Loud of the chase, and low of love.

'O Love! art thou a silver fish,
Shy of the line and shy of gaffing,
Which we do follow, fierce, yet laughing
Casting at thee the light-winged wish?
And at the last shall we bring thee up
From the crystal darkness under the cup
Of lily folden,
On broad leaves golden?

'O Love! art thou a silver deer?
Swift thy starred feet as wing of swallow,
While we with rushing arrows follow:

And at the last shall we draw near,

And over thy velvet neck cast thongs,

Woven of roses, of stars, of songs,

New chains all moulden

Of rare gems olden?'

They hung the slaughtered fish like swords

On saplings slender; like scimitars

Bright, and ruddied from new-dead wars,

Blazed in the light the scaly hordes.

They piled up boughs beneath the trees,

AN INDIAN ENCAMPMENT ON A RIVER BY THOMAS MOWER MARTIN, 1881-1931.

Of cedar-web and green fir tassel;
Low did the pointed pine tops rustle,
The camp fire blushed to the tender breeze.

The hounds laid dew-laps on the ground,
With needles of pine sweet, soft and rusty,
Dreamed of the dead stag stout and lusty;
A bat by the red flames wove its round.

The darkness built its wigwam walls
Close round the camp, and at its curtain
Pressed shapes, thin woven and uncertain,
As white locks of tall waterfalls.

MARY COLBORNE-VEEL (BORN C. 1850)

Little is known of this Australian poet, except that she published a collection entitled The Fairest of the Angels and Other Verse *in 1894. This is the only poem of hers that appears in later anthologies, but its eerie charm earns it a place here.*

SONG OF THE TREES

We are the Trees.
Our dark and leafy glade
Bands the bright earth with softer mysteries.
Beneath us changed and tamed the seasons run:

In burning zones, we build against the sun
Long centuries of shade.

We are the Trees,
Who grow for man's desire,
Heat in our faithful hearts, and fruits that please.
Dwelling beneath our tents, he lightly gains
The few sufficiencies his life attains –
Shelter, and food, and fire.

We are the Trees
That by great waters stand,
By rills that murmur to our murmuring bees.
And where, in tracts all desolate and waste,
The palm-foot stays, man follows on, to taste
Springs in the desert sand.

We are the Trees
Who travel where he goes
Over the vast, inhuman, wandering seas.
His tutors we, in that adventure brave –
He launched with us upon the untried wave,
And now its mastery knows.

We are the Trees
Who bear him company
In life and death. His happy sylvan case
He wins through us; through us, his cities spread
That like a forest guard his unfenced head
'Gainst storm and bitter sky.

We are the Trees.

On us the dying rest

Their strange, sad eyes, in farewell messages.

And we, his comrades still, since earth began,

Wave mournful boughs above the grave of man,

And coffin his cold breast.

FANNY PARNELL (1854-1882)

One of the many politically motivated Irish writers, Fanny Parnell was the sister of Charles Stewart Parnell, the great advocate of Irish Home Rule and president of the Irish National Land League, which advocated radical reform of the laws concerning land ownership. Actively involved in her brother's work, Fanny wrote fiery poems and articles in The Nation *and other newspapers in support of their cause.*

AFTER DEATH

Shall mine eyes behold thy glory, O my country?

Shall mine eyes behold thy glory?

Or shall the darkness close around them, ere the sunblaze

Break at last upon thy story?

When the nations ope for thee their queenly circle,

As a sweet new sister hail thee,

Shall these lips be sealed in callous death and silence,

That have known but to bewail thee?

Shall the ear be deaf that only loved thy praises,
When all men their tribute bring thee?
Shall the mouth be clay that sang thee in thy squalor
When all poets' mouths shall sing thee?

Ah! the harpings and the salvos and the shoutings
Of thy exiled sons returning!
I should hear, tho' dead and mouldered, and the grave-damps
Should not chill my bosom's burning.

Ah! the tramp of feet victorious! I should hear them
'Mid the shamrocks and the mosses,
And my heart should toss within the shroud and quiver,
As a captive dreamer tosses.

I should, turn and rend the cere-clothes round me,
Giant sinews I should borrow –
Crying, 'O, my brothers, I have also loved her
In her loneliness and sorrow!

'Let me join with you the jubilant procession;
Let me chant with you her story;
Then contented I shall go back to the shamrocks,
Now mine eyes have seen her glory!'

કળ

E. Nesbit (1858-1924)

Edith Nesbit is best known as the author of The Railway Children *and other cosy children's classics, so it often comes as a surprise to discover that she spent much of her adult life in an unconventional* ménage à trois *in South London and was at one stage the lover of George Bernard Shaw. Her poems are distinguished by their endearing no-nonsense tone. It may be interesting to compare the last lines of 'Among His Books' with Wendy Cope's 'Defining the Problem' (see page 148), written almost a century later.*

Among His Books

A silent room – gray with a dusty blight
Of loneliness;
A room with not enough of life or light
Its form to dress.

Books enough though! The groaning sofa bears
A goodly store
Books on the window-seat, and on the chairs,
And on the floor.

Books of all sorts of soul, all sorts of age,
All sorts of face
Black-letter, vellum, and the flimsy page
Of commonplace.

All bindings, from the cloth whose hue distracts
One's weary nerves,
To yellow parchment, binding rare old tracts
It serves – deserves.

Books on the shelves, and in the cupboard books,
Worthless and rare –
Books on the mantelpiece – where'er one looks
Books everywhere!

Books! books! the only things in life I find
Not wholly vain.
Books in my hands – books in my heart enshrined
Books in my brain.

My friends are they: for children and for wife
They serve me too;
For these alone, of all dear things in life,
Have I found true.

They do not flatter, change, deny, deceive
Ah no – not they!
The same editions which one night you leave
You find next day.

You don't find railway novels where you left
Your Elzevirs!
Your Aldines don't betray you – leave bereft
Your lonely years!

And yet this common book of Common Prayer
My heart prefers,
Because the names upon the fly-leaf there
Are mine and hers.

It's a dead flower that makes it open so –
Forget-me-not
The Marriage Service…well, my dear, you know
Who first forgot.

Those were the days when in the choir we two
Sat – used to sing
When I believed in God, in love, in you
In everything.

Through quiet lanes to church we used to come,
Happy and good,
Clasp hands through sermon, and go slowly home
Down through the wood.

Kisses? A certain yellow rose no doubt
That porch still shows,
Whenever I hear kisses talked about.
I smell that rose!

No – I don't blame you – since you only proved
My choice unwise,
And taught me books should trusted be and loved,
Not lips and eyes!

And so I keep your book – your flower – to show
How much I care
For the dear memory of what, you know,
You never were.

THE WIFE OF ALL AGES

I do not catch these subtle shades of feeling,
Your fine distinctions are too fine for me;
This meeting, scheming, longing, trembling, dreaming,
To me mean love, and only love, you see;
In me at least 'tis love, you will admit,
And you the only man who wakens it.

Suppose I yearned, and longed, and dreamed, and fluttered,
What would you say or think, or further, do?
Why should one rule be fit for me to follow,
While there exists a different law for you?
If all these fires and fancies came my way,
Would you believe love was so far away?

On all these other women – never doubt it –
'Tis love you lavish, love you promised me!
What do I care to be the first, or fiftieth?
It is the *only one* I care to be.
Dear, I would be your sun, as mine you are,
Not the most radiant wonder of a star.

And so, good-bye! Among such sheaves of roses
You will not miss the flower I take from you;
Amid the music of so many voices
You will forget the little songs I knew –
The foolish tender words I used to say,
The little common sweets of every day.

BY THE WINDOW BY SIR JOHN CARLSEN, 1851-1931.

The world, no doubt, has fairest fruits and blossoms
To give to you: but what, ah! what for me?
Nay, after all I am your slave and bondmaid,
And all my world is in my slavery.
So, as before, I welcome any part
Which you may choose to give me of your heart.

AMY LEVY (1861- 1889)

In the course of her short life Amy Levy became well known as both a poet and a novelist with an interest in feminism and in Jewish issues, though she offended many Jews with her controversial novel Reuben Sachs. *Always prone to periods of melancholy, she committed suicide at the age of twenty-seven.*

A BALLAD OF RELIGION AND MARRIAGE

Swept into limbo is the host
Of heavenly angels, row on row;
The Father, Son, and Holy Ghost,
Pale and defeated, rise and go.
The great Jehovah is laid low,
Vanished his burning bush and rod –
Say, are we doomed to deeper woe?
Shall marriage go the way of God?

Monogamous, still at our post,
Reluctantly we undergo

Domestic round of boiled and roast,
Yet deem the whole proceeding slow.
Daily the secret murmurs grow;
We are no more content to plod
Along the beaten paths – and so
Marriage must go the way of God.

Soon, before all men, each shall toast
The seven strings unto his bow,
Like beacon fires along the coast,
The flames of love shall glance and glow.
Nor let nor hindrance man shall know,
From natal bath to funeral sod;
Perennial shall his pleasures flow
When marriage goes the way of God.

Grant, in a million years at most,
Folk shall be neither pairs nor odd –
Alas! we shan't be there to boast
'Marriage has gone the way of God!'

A LONDON PLANE-TREE

Green is the plane-tree in the square,
The other trees are brown;
They droop and pine for country air,
The plane-tree loves the town.

Here from my garret-pane I mark
The plane-tree bud and blow,
Shed her recuperative bark,
And spread her shade below.

Among her branches, in and out,
The city breezes play;
The dull fog wraps her round about;
Above, the smoke curls grey.

Others the country take for choice,
And hold the town in scorn;
But she has listen'd to the voice
On city breezes borne.

ॐ♠ॐ

MARY ELIZABETH COLERIDGE (1861-1907)

*The great-great niece of Samuel Taylor Coleridge, Mary Elizabeth had published
a novel and a number of essays before the poet Robert Bridges became aware of
her verse and encouraged her to publish it, too. These two poems reflect the
passion for romanticism and the supernatural she shared with her
more famous relative.*

A MOMENT

The clouds had made a crimson crown
Above the mountains high.

The stormy sun was going down
In a stormy sky.

Why did you let your eyes so rest on me,
And hold your breath between?
In all the ages this can never be
As if it had not been.

UNWELCOME

We were young, we were merry, we were very very wise,
And the door stood open at our feast,
When there passed us a woman with the West in her eyes,
And a man with his back to the East.

Oh, still grew the hearts that were beating so fast,
The loudest voice was still.
The jest died away on our lips as they passed,
And the rays of July struck chill.

The cups of red wine turned pale on the board,
The white bread black as soot.
The hound forgot the hand of her lord,
She fell down at his foot.

Low let me lie, where the dead dog lies,
Ere I sit me down again at a feast,

When there passes a woman with the West in her eyes,
And a man with his back to the East.

DORA SIGERSON SHORTER (1866-1917)

Another politically motivated Irish poem: the sixteen dead men are those who were hanged for their part in the Easter Rebellion of 1916, an episode that remains fresh in the minds of Irish patriots.

SIXTEEN DEAD MEN

Hark! in the still night. Who goes there?
'Fifteen dead men.' Why do they wait?
'Hasten, comrade, death is so fair.'
Now comes their Captain through the dim gate.

Sixteen dead men! What on their sword?
'A nation's honour proud do they bear.'
What on their bent heads? 'God's holy word
All of their nation's heart blended in prayer.'

Sixteen dead men! What makes their shroud?
'All of their nation's love wraps them around.'
Where do their bodies lie, brave and so proud?
'Under the gallows-tree in prison ground.'

MUCKROSS BAY, KILLARNEY, DONEGAL BY ALEXANDER WILLIAMS, 1846-1930.

Sixteen dead men! Where do they go?
'To join their regiment, where Sarsfield leads;
Wolfe Tone and Emmet, too, well do they know.
There shall they bivouac, telling great deeds.'

Sixteen dead men! Shall they return?
'Yea, they shall come again, – breath of our breath.
They on our nation's hearth made old fires burn.
Guard her unconquered soul, strong in their death.'

ETHNA CARBERY (1866-1902)

The supernatural is never far away in Irish poetry, though this poem may simply be a warning to young women to be careful of their virtue!

THE LOVE-TALKER

I met the Love-Talker one eve in the glen,
He was handsomer than any of our handsome young men,
His eyes were blacker than the sloe, his voice sweeter far
Than the crooning of old Kevin's pipes beyond in Coolnagar.

I was bound for the milking with a heart fair and free –
My grief! my grief! that bitter hour drained the life from me;
I thought him human lover, though his lips on mine were cold,
And the breath of death blew keen on me within his hold.

I know not what way he came, no shadow fell behind,
But all the sighing rushes swayed beneath a fairy wind;
The thrush ceased its singing, a mist crept about,
We two clung together – with the world shut out.

Beyond the ghostly mist I could hear my cattle low,
The little cow from Ballina, clean as driven snow,
The dun cow from Kerry, the roan from Inisheer,
Oh, pitiful their calling – and his whispers in my ear!

His eyes were a fire; his words were a snare;
I cried my mother's name, but no help was there;
I made the blessed Sign – then he gave a dreary moan,
A wisp of cloud went floating by, and I stood alone.

Running ever thro' my head is an old-time rune – .
'Who meets the Love-Talker must weave her shroud soon.'
My mother's face is furrowed with the salt tears that fall,
But the kind eyes of my father are the saddest sight of all.

I have spun the fleecy lint and now my wheel is still,
The linen length is woven for my shroud fine and chill,
I shall stretch me on the bed where a happy maid I lay –
Pray for the soul of Maire Og at dawning of the day!

❧❧❧

CHARLOTTE MEW (1869-1928)

Although older than the more famous members of the Bloomsbury set, Charlotte Mew lived on the fringes of that circle and her verse was well-known in the years before the First World War. Thomas Hardy called her 'the least pretentious but undoubtedly the best woman poet of our day'. Her life was blighted by tragedy – two of her siblings became mentally ill, a circumstance that led her and her sister Anne to avoid marriage in case the disease was passed on to their children; Anne subsequently died of cancer and Charlotte took her own life the following year.

THE CALL

From our low seat beside the fire
Where we have dozed and dreamed and watched the glow
Or raked the ashes, stopping so
We scarcely saw the sun or rain
Above, or looked much higher
Than this same quiet red or burned-out fire.
To-night we heard a call,
A rattle on the window-pane,
A voice on the sharp air,
And felt a breath stirring our hair,
A flame within us: Something swift and tall
Swept in and out and that was all.
Was it a bright or a dark angel? Who can know?
It left no mark upon the snow,
But suddenly it snapped the chain
Unbarred, flung wide the door
Which will not shut again;

And so we cannot sit here any more.

We must arise and go:

The world is cold without

And dark and hedged about

With mystery and enmity and doubt,

But we must go

Though yet we do not know

Who called, or what marks we shall leave upon the snow.

Eva Gore-Booth (1870-1926)

Eva Gore-Booth was the sister of the famous Irish patriot Countess Constance Markiewicz, the first woman to be elected as a Member of Parliament to Westminster, although she never took her seat. Like her sister, Eva was deeply involved in politics and in social work on behalf of women. Her most famous poem, however, is this touching piece of nostalgia inspired by her childhood home in County Sligo.

The Little Waves of Breffny

The grand road from the mountain goes shining to the sea;

And there is traffic in it and many a horse and cart,

But the little roads of Cloonagh are dearer far to me,

And the little roads of Cloonagh go rambling through my heart.

A great storm from the ocean goes shouting o'er the hill,

And there is glory in it and terror on the wind,

But the haunted air of twilight is very strange and still,
And the little winds of twilight are dearer to my mind.

The great waves of the Atlantic sweep storming on the way,
Shining green and silver with the hidden herring shoal,
But the Little Waves of Breffny have drenched my heart in spray,
And the Little Waves of Breffny go stumbling through my soul.

MARIANNE MOORE (1887-1972)

One of the most acclaimed American poets of her generation, Marianne Moore was born in St Louis and later moved to New York. She is considered one of the founders of American Modernism.

TO A SNAIL

If 'compression is the first grace of style',
you have it. Contractility is a virtue
as modesty is a virtue.
It is not the acquisition of any one thing
that is able to adorn,
or the incidental quality that occurs
as a concomitant of something well said,
that we value in style,
but the principle that is hid:
in the absence of feet, 'a method of conclusions';
'a knowledge of principles',
in the curious phenomenon of your occipital horn.

IN THE GARDEN BY MARIE FIRMIN-GIRARD, 1838-1921.

SILENCE

My father used to say,
'Superior people never make long visits,
have to be shown Longfellow's grave
or the glass flowers at Harvard.
Self-reliant like the cat –
that takes its prey to privacy,
the mouse's limp tail hanging like a shoelace from its mouth –
they sometimes enjoy solitude,
and can be robbed of speech
by speech which has delighted them.
The deepest feeling always shows itself in silence;
not in silence, but restraint.'
Nor was he insincere in saying, 'Make my house your inn.'
Inns are not residences.

DOROTHY PARKER (1893-1967)

A founder member of the Algonquin Club, the élite New York literary circle of the 1920s, Dorothy Parker was notorious for her acerbic wit, which she could turn on herself as well as against others: at her seventieth birthday party she is said to have remarked, 'If I had any decency I'd be dead. Most of my friends are.' Although her writing – which includes many sparkling essays as well as poems – covers a wide range of subjects, she frequently returned to the sorrows of love and the inadequacies of men. It may be interesting to compare this poem with Wendy Cope's 'Flowers' (see page 149).

ONE PERFECT ROSE

A single flow'r he sent me, since we met.
All tenderly his messenger he chose;
Deep-hearted, pure, with scented dew still wet
One perfect rose.

I knew the language of the floweret;
'My fragile leaves,' it said, 'his heart enclose.'
Love long has taken for his amulet
One perfect rose.

Why is it no one ever sent me yet
One perfect limousine, do you suppose?
Ah no, it's always just my luck to get
One perfect rose.

STEVIE SMITH (1902-1971)

'Not Waving But Drowning' is the title poem of Stevie Smith's most famous
collection of poems. Born in Hull, she lived most of her life in London
with a beloved aunt. Although she often wrote about loneliness and death,
the tone of her work varied greatly, from the witty to the whimsical. She once
remarked that she found death 'the most exciting thing' and wondered
why people grumbled so much about old age.

NOT WAVING BUT DROWNING

Nobody heard him, the dead man,
But still he lay moaning:
I was much further out than you thought
And not waving but drowning.

Poor chap, he always loved larking
And now he's dead
It must have been too cold for him his heart gave way,
They said.

Oh, no no no, it was too cold always
(Still the dead one lay moaning)
I was much too far out all my life
And not waving but drowning.

COME, DEATH (1)

Why dost thou dally, Death, and tarry on the way?
When I have summoned thee with prayers and tears, why dost thou stay?
Come, Death, and carry now my soul away.

Wilt thou not come for calling, must I show
Force to constrain thy quick attention to my woe?
I have a hand upon thy Coat, and will
Not let thee go.

How foolish are the words of the old monks,
In Life remember Death.
Who would forget
Thou closer hangst on every finished breath?
How vain the work of Christianity
To teach humanity
Courage in its mortality.
Who would not rather die
And quiet lie
Beneath the sod
With or without a god?

Foolish illusion, what has Life to give?
Why should man more fear Death than fear to live?

COME, DEATH (2)

I feel ill. What can the matter be?
I'd ask God to have pity on me,
But I turn to the one I know, and say:
Come, Death, and carry me away.

Ah me, sweet Death, you are the only god
Who comes as a servant when he is called, you know,
Listen then to this sound I make, it is sharp,
Come, Death. Do not be slow.

ANNE MORROW LINDBERGH (1906-2001)

Anne Morrow married the pioneer aviator Charles Lindbergh and had the distinction of being the first woman in America to obtain a glider pilot's licence. Left to herself she would have shunned the limelight, but her husband's achievements and then the kidnapping and murder of their baby thrust her into the public eye throughout the 1920s and '30s, when the Lindberghs took refuge in Europe. Anne continued to write throughout her life, drawing largely on her own personal experiences.

HEIGHT

When I was young I felt so small
And frightened for the world was tall.

And even grasses seemed to me
A forest of immensity.

Until I learned that I could grow,
A glance would leave them far below.

Spanning a tree's height with my eye,
Suddenly I soared as high,

And fixing on a star I grew,
I pushed my head against the blue!

Still, like a singing lark, I find
Rapture to leave the grass behind.

OPPOSITE. CONWAY BY JOSEPH KNIGHT, 1837-1909.

And sometimes standing in a crowd
My lips are cool against a cloud.

MAYA ANGELOU (1928–)

The first volume of Maya Angelou's autobiography, I Know Why the Caged Bird Sings, *published in 1969, brought her immediate international acclaim. Since then she has become known as a poet and a tireless campaigner for the rights of black people, and has been awarded a Pulitzer Prize. 'Still I Rise' perfectly reflects her indomitable spirit.*

STILL I RISE

You may write me down in history
With your bitter, twisted lies,
You may trod me in the very dirt
But still, like dust, I'll rise.

Does my sassiness upset you?
Why are you beset with gloom?
'Cause I walk like I've got oil wells
Pumping in my living room.

Just like moons and like suns,
With the certainty of tides,
Just like hopes springing high,
Still I'll rise.

OPPOSITE. L'OFFRANDE BY TSHIBOKO MPUTU KABONGO (BORN 1948).

Did you want to see me broken?
Bowed head and lowered eyes?
Shoulders filling down like teardrops,
Weakened by my soulful cries.

Does my haughtiness offend you?
Don't you take it awful hard
'Cause I laugh like I've got gold mines
Diggin' in my own back yard.

You may shoot me with your words,
You may cut me with your eyes,
You may kill me with your hatefulness,
But still, like air, I'll rise.

Does my sexiness upset you?
Does it come as a surprise
That I dance like I've got diamonds
At the meeting of my thighs?

Out of the huts of history's shame
I rise
Up from a past that's rooted in pain
I rise
I'm a black ocean, leaping and wide,
Welling and swelling I bear in the tide.

Leaving behind nights of terror and fear
I rise
Into a daybreak that's wondrously clear

I rise

Bringing the gifts that my ancestors gave,

I am the dream and the hope of the slave.

I rise

I rise

I rise.

ADRIENNE RICH (1929–)

Adrienne Rich's most recent books of poetry are Midnight Salvage: Poems 1995-1998 and Fox: Poems 1998-2000. *A new selection of her essays,* Arts of the Possible: Essays and Conversations, *was published in 2001. She has recently been the recipient of the Dorothea Tanning Prize of the Academy of American Poets 'for mastery in the art of poetry' and the Lannan Foundation Lifetime Achievement Award. She lives in California.*

LIVING IN SIN

She had thought the studio would keep itself;

no dust upon the furniture of love.

Half heresy, to wish the taps less vocal,

the panes relieved of grime. A plate of pears,

a piano with a Persian shawl, a cat

stalking the picturesque amusing mouse

had risen at his urging.

Not that at five each separate stair would writhe

under the milkman's tramp; that morning light

so coldly would delineate the scraps

of last night's cheese and three sepulchral bottles;

that on the kitchen shelf among the saucers

a pair of beetle-eyes would fix her own –

envoy from some village in the moldings . . .

Meanwhile, he, with a yawn,

sounded a dozen notes upon the keyboard,

declared it out of tune, shrugged at the mirror,

rubbed at his beard, went out for cigarettes;

while she, jeered by the minor demons,

pulled back the sheets and made the bed and found

a towel to dust the table-top,

and let the coffee-pot boil over on the stove.

By evening she was back in love again,

though not so wholly but throughout the night

she woke sometimes to feel the daylight coming

like a relentless milkman up the stairs.

SYLVIA PLATH (1932-1963)

American-born Sylvia Plath met the future Poet Laureate Ted Hughes in Cambridge, England, where she was studying on a Fulbright scholarship. They married in 1956, but he left her and their two children in 1962. Already a victim of mental instability, she took her own life the following year. Many of her best poems were written in these last unhappy months and greatly enhanced her posthumous reputation.

SPINSTER

Now this particular girl
During a ceremonious April walk
With her latest suitor
Found herself, of a sudden, intolerably struck
By the birds' irregular babel
And the leaves' litter.

By this tumult afflicted, she
Observed her lover's gestures unbalance the air,
His gait stray uneven
Through a rank wilderness of fern and flower.
She judged petals in disarray,
The whole season, sloven.

How she longed for winter then!
Scrupulously austere in its order
Of white and black
Ice and rock, each sentiment within border,
And heart's frosty discipline
Exact as a snowflake.

But here – a burgeoning

Unruly enough to pitch her five queenly wits

Into vulgar motley

A treason not to be borne.

Let idiots

Reel giddy in bedlam spring:

She withdrew neatly.

And round her house she set

Such a barricade of barb and check

Against mutinous weather

As no mere insurgent man could hope to break

With curse, fist, threat

Or love, either.

MIRROR

I am silver and exact. I have no preconceptions.

Whatever I see I swallow immediately

Just as it is, unmisted by love or dislike.

I am not cruel, only truthful –

The eye of a little god, four-cornered.

Most of the time I meditate on the opposite wall.

It is pink, with speckles. I have looked at it so long

I think it is a part of my heart. But it flickers.

Faces and darkness separate us over and over.

Now I am a lake. A woman bends over me,

Searching my reaches for what she really is.

Then she turns to those liars, the candles or the moon.

I see her back, and reflect it faithfully.

She rewards me with tears and an agitation of hands.

I am important to her. She comes and goes.

Each morning it is her face that replaces the darkness.

In me she has drowned a young girl, and in me an old woman

Rises toward her day after day, like a terrible fish.

NEAR SORRENTO BY JOHN BRETT, 1830-1902.

ROSEMARY TONKS (1932–)

In her youth Rosemary Tonks was a prolific author, producing novels for both adults and children as well as collections of verse. She converted to Christianity in the 1970s, since when she seems not to have published any further writings.

STORY OF A HOTEL ROOM

Thinking we were safe – insanity!
We went to make love. All the same
Idiots to trust the little hotel bedroom
Then in the gloom......
......And who does not know that pair of shutters
With the awkward hook on them
All screeching whispers? Very well then, in the gloom
We set about acquiring one another
Urgently! But on a temporary basis
Only as guests – just guests of one another's senses.

But idiots to feel so safe you hold back nothing
Because the bed of cold, electric linen
Happens to be illicit...
To make love as well as that is ruinous.
Londoner, Parisian, someone should have warned us
That without permanent intentions
You have absolutely no protection
– If the act is clean, authentic, sumptuous,
The concurring deep love of the heart
Follows the naked work, profoundly moved by it.

WOMEN'S POETRY

FLEUR ADCOCK (1934–)

*Born in New Zealand, Fleur Adcock has lived in Britain since 1963.
In addition to her own writing she has translated the work of Rumanian
poets and is the editor of* The Oxford Book of Contemporary
New Zealand Poetry *and* The Faber Book of Twentieth Century
Women's Poetry. *Her poetry is often ironic in tone and domestic in
theme, but sometimes – as in this poem – she draws on experiences
from her extensive travels.*

SUMMER IN BUCHAREST

We bought raspberries in the market;
but raspberries are discredited:

they sag in their bag, fermenting
into a froth of suspect juice.
And strawberries are seriously compromised:
a taint – you must have heard the stories.

As for the red currants, well, they say
the only real red currants are dead.

(Don't you believe it: the fields are full of them,
swelling hopefully on their twigs,

and the dead ones weren't red anyway
but some mutation of black or white.)

143

We thought of choosing gooseberries,
until we heard they'd been infiltrated

by raspberries in gooseberry jackets.
You can't tell what to trust these days.

There are dates, they say, but they're imported;
and its still too early for the grape harvest.

All we can do is wait and hope.
It's been a sour season for fruit.

MARGARET ATWOOD (1939–)

Canada's foremost novelist – the author of The Handmaid's Tale, Alias Grace,
The Robber Bride *and many others – was finally awarded Britain's Booker Prize
for Fiction in 2000 for* The Blind Assassin. *She has always had a parallel
career as a poet, often concentrating, as in her novels,
on 'women's issues'.*

A WOMEN'S ISSUE

The woman in the spiked device
that locks around the waist and between the legs,
with holes in it like a tea strainer
is Exhibit A.

The woman in black with a net window
to see through and a four-inch wooden peg
jammed up between her legs so she can't be raped
is Exhibit B.

Exhibit C is the young girl
dragged into the bush by the midwives
and made to sing while they scrape the flesh
from between her legs, then tie her thighs
till she scabs over and is called healed.
Now she can be married.
For each childbirth they'll cut her
open, then sew her up.
Men like tight women.
The ones that die are carefully buried.

The next exhibit lies flat on her back
while eighty men a night
move through her, ten an hour.
She looks at the ceiling, listens
to the door open and close.
A bell keeps ringing.
Nobody knows how she got here.

You'll notice that what they have in common
is between the legs. Is this
why wars are fought?

Enemy territory, no man's
land, to be entered furtively,

fenced, owned but never surely,

scene of these desperate forays

at midnight, captures

and sticky murders, doctors' rubber gloves

greasy with blood, flesh made inert, the surge

of your own uneasy power.

This is no museum.

Who invented the word love?

SHARON OLDS (1942–)

One of the strongest poetic voices to have emerged from the feminist movement, Sharon Olds has also written of paying attention to 'the small beauties of the physical world – as if it were our duty to find things to love, to bind ourselves to this world.'

THE CONNOISSEUSE OF SLUGS

When I was a connoisseuse of slugs

I would part the ivy leaves, and look for the

naked jelly of those gold bodies,

translucent strangers glistening along the

stones, slowly, their gelatinous bodies

at my mercy. Made mostly of water, they would shrivel

to nothing if they were sprinkled with salt,

but I was not interested in that. What I liked

was to draw aside the ivy, breathe the

Telle Mère, telle Fille by Ndoki Kitekutu, born 1949

odor of the wall, and stand there in silence
until the slug forgot I was there
and sent its antennae up out of its
head, the glimmering umber horns
rising like telescopes, until finally the
sensitive knobs would pop out the ends,
delicate and intimate. Years later,
when I first saw a naked man,
I gasped with pleasure to see that
quiet mystery reenacted, the slow
elegant being coming out of hiding and
gleaming in the dark air, eager and so
trusting you could weep.

WENDY COPE (1945–)

Wendy Cope is perhaps the wittiest poet of her generation,
with her uniquely jaundiced views on life, love and men. Her collections include
Making Cocoa for Kingsley Amis *and* Serious Concerns.

DEFINING THE PROBLEM

I can't forgive you. Even if I could,
You wouldn't pardon me for seeing through you.
And yet I cannot cure myself of love
For what I thought you were before I knew you.

FLOWERS

Some men never think of it.
You did. You'd come along
And say you'd nearly brought me flowers
But something had gone wrong.

The shop was closed. Or you had doubts –
The sort that minds like ours
Dream up incessantly. You thought
I might not want your flowers.

It made me smile and hug you then.
Now I can only smile.
But, look, the flowers you nearly brought
Have lasted all this while.

MICHELE ROBERTS (1949-)

Michele Roberts has been an important writer and broadcaster since her novel
Daughters of the House *was shortlisted for the Booker Prize in 1992.*
She has been described as 'one of the most original writers to emerge
from the Women's Movement'.

MAGNIFICAT

(For Sian, after thirteen years)

Oh this man
what a meal he made of me
how he chewed and gobbled and sucked
in the end he spat me all out

you arrived on the dot, in the nick
of time, with your red curls flying
I was about to slip down the sink like grease
I nearly collapsed, I almost
wiped myself out like a stain
I called for you, and you came, you voyaged
fierce as a small archangel with swords and breasts
you declared the birth of a new life
in my kitchen there was an annunciation
and I was still, awed by your hair's glory

you commanded me to sing of my redemption
oh my friend, how
you were mother for me, and how

I could let myself lean on you
comfortable as an old cloth
familiar as enamel saucepans
I was a child again, pyjama'ed
in winceyette, my hair plaited, and you

listened, you soothed me like cake and milk
you listened to me for three days, and I poured
it out, I flowed all over you like wine, like oil
you touched the place where it hurt
at night, we slept together in my big bed
your shoulder eased me towards dreams

when we met, I tell you
it was a birthday party, a funeral
it was a holy communion
between women, a Visitation
it was two old she-goats butting
and nuzzling each other in the smelly fold

CAROL ANN DUFFY (1955–)

Carol Ann Duffy has been described as 'in many ways the characteristic
English poet of the Eighties and Nineties'. Much of her work is political,
though this example – like the poems of so many of her contemporaries – takes
a bitter-sweet slant on modern love.

VALENTINE

Not a red rose or a satin heart.
I give you an onion.
It is a moon wrapped in brown paper.
It promises light
like the careful undressing of love.

Here.
It will blind you with tears
like a lover.
It will make your reflection
a wobbling photo of grief.

I am trying to be truthful.
Not a cute card or a kissogram.

I give you an onion.
Its fierce kiss will stay on your lips,
possessive and faithful
as we are,
for as long as we are.

Take it.
Its platinum loops shrink to a wedding-ring
if you like.
Lethal.
Its scent will cling to your fingers,
cling to your knife.

INDEX OF FIRST LINES

Acknowledgements

Pictures:

Front cover: *Portrait of the Artist's Wife, Wilhelmina Begas*, 1828 (oil on canvas) by Karl Joseph Begas (1794-1854). Nationalgalerie, Berlin, Germany / Bildarchiv Steffens / Bridgeman Art Library

Poems:

'Summer in Bucharest' from *Poems 1960-2000* by **Fleur Adcock**, by permission of Bloodaxe Books, 2000. 'Still I rise'by **Maya Angelou**, taken from the Virago Press edition, pub. by arrangement with Random House Inc. Copyright 1978 Maya Angelou. Reprinted by permission of Time Warner Books UK and of Random House Inc.: 'Still I Rise', from *And Still I Rise* by Maya Angelou, copyright © 1978 by Maya Angelou. 'A Women's Issues' by **Margaret Atwood** from the collection *True Stories*, © 1981 Reprinted by permission of Curtis Brown Ltd, London on behalf of Margaret Atwood. Currently published in the United States in *Selected Poems II*, Houghton Mifflin Co. © 1987, and in Canada in *Selected Poems 1964-1984* by Oxford University Press, © 1990. Reprinted by permission of the Author. 'Defining the Problem' and 'Flowers' from *Serious concerns* by **Wendy Cope** are reprinted by permission of Faber and Faber Limited and of PFD on behalf of Wendy Cope. 'Valentine' from *Mean Time* by **Carol Ann Duffy**, published by Anvil Press Poetry in 1993. 'Height' by **Anne Morrow Lindbergh**. Reprinted by permission of Charles Scribner's Sons, a division of Simon & Schuster, Inc. 'To a Snail 'and 'Silence' by **Marianne Moore**, reprinted with the permission of Faber and Faber Ltd and of Simon & Schuster, Inc from *The Collected Poems of Marianne Moore* by Marianne Moore. Copyright © 1935 by Marianne Moore, copyright renewed © 1963 by Marianne Moore and T.S. Eliot. The Connoisseuse of Slugs' from *The Dead and the Living* by **Sharon Olds**, copyright © 1987 by Sharon Olds. Used by permission of Alfred A. Knopf, a division of Random House, Inc. 'One Perfect Rose' by **Dorothy Parker**, reprinted by permission of Gerald Duckworth & Co. Ltd and by permission of Viking Penguin, a division of Penguin Putnam Inc: "One Perfect Rose", copyright 1926, renewed © by Dorothy Parker, from *The Portable Dorothy Parker*, edited by Brendan Gill. 'Spinster' and 'Mirror' from *Collected Poems* by **Sylvia Platt**. Reprinted by permission of Faber and Faber Limited and of Harper Collins, Inc. 'Living in Sin'. Copyright © 1993, 1955 by **Adrienne Rich**, from *Collected Early Poems:1950-1970* by Adrienne Rich. Used by permission of the author and W.W. Norton and Company, Inc. 'Magnificat' from *All the Selves I was* by **Michèle Roberts** Copyright © 1995 Michèle Roberts. 'Come Death' and 'Not Waving, but Drowning' by **Stevie Smith**, from *Collected Poems of Stevie Smith*, copyright © 1972 by Stevie Smith. Reprinted by permission of the Estate of James MacGibbon and New Directions Publishing Corp. 'Story of a Hotel Room' from *Notes on Cafés and Bedrooms* by **Rosemary Tonks**. Reprinted by permission of the publishers and of Sheil Land Associates Ltd.

Although every effort has been made to trace the copyright holders. The editor apologizes for any omission which may have occurred.